GAME DAY
NOTRE DAME FOOTBALL

1987 Heisman
Trophy winner
Tim Brown

GAME DAY
NOTRE DAME FOOTBALL

*The Greatest Games, Players, Coaches and Teams
in the Glorious Tradition of Fighting Irish Football*

TRIUMPH
B O O K S
CHICAGO

Athlon® Sports
AMERICA'S PREMIER SPORTS ANNUALS

Library of Congress Control Number: 2006903358

This book is available in quantity at special discounts for your group or organization. For further information, contact:

Triumph Books
542 South Dearborn Street
Suite 750
Chicago, Illinois 60605
(312) 939-3330
Fax (312) 663-3557

CONTRIBUTING WRITER: Kevin Daniels

EDITOR: Rob Doster

PHOTO EDITOR: Tim Clark
PHOTO ASSISTANT: Danny Murphy

DESIGN: Anderson Thomas Design
PRODUCTION: Odds & Ends Multimedia

PHOTO CREDITS: Athlon Sports Archive, AP/Wide World Photos, Blue & Gold Illustrated, Getty Images, Bettmen/Corbis, University of Notre Dame, Matt Cashore

Printed in U.S.A.

ISBN-13: 978-1-57243-881-1
ISBN-10: 1-57243-881-9

CONTENTS

Foreword

I find that when I return to Notre Dame for a football weekend or a summer camp with my kids, a wave of emotion and pride hits me more and more. I truly believe there is no middle ground with ND—people either love it or hate it. This is one of the reasons ND is *the* most recognized university in the land, bar none, and has the richest football tradition.

I'm proud to say that I got to enjoy more than the normal four years at Notre Dame. I actually went there for 10 straight years—1975–1985—and it gave me great perspective, first as a wide-eyed 11-year-old watching my older brother Bob win a national championship with ND greats like Joe Montana, Ken McAfee, Ross Browner and a host of others. Then I got to see the university through 18-year-old eyes, as my brother Greg attended school there, right before I went there myself and lived my dream of playing at Notre Dame, while also meeting my wife there.

So as I grew up on ND, I saw the thousands who went there, and the millions who cheered for our teams. A lot of those fans are subway alumni from the northwest to the southeast and everywhere in between. These are people who never went to school at Notre

Dame, but root for it and live it, like they attended this great university themselves. This is another of the reasons that ND is set apart from all others.

The athletic achievements are well-documented in the following pages. Enjoy them, and after you read them you will understand why, when the name Notre Dame is brought up in conversation, it is talked about with respect. Even with my nine years in the NFL, there has been no feeling I've had in sports better than running out of the tunnel at Notre Dame wearing that gold helmet. I look back on my years as a dream come true and look forward to the years ahead as Notre Dame continues to be the great university it has been. Along with all my former teammates and classmates, I say the words that make me incredibly proud: "We are ND."

—Mike Golic

Introduction

Notre Dame has won football games at a higher rate than any other school in intercollegiate competition. It's not surprising, then, that the two winningest coaches in college football history presided over the Notre Dame football program. Knute Rockne, a Notre Dame alumnus (class of 1914) coached at his alma mater for 13 years (1918–1930) and was 105–12–5 for a winning percentage of .881, the highest in history. Frank Leahy, who played for Rockne at Notre Dame, went 87–11–9 in his 11 years (1941–1943, 1946–1953) under the Golden Dome, for an .855 average, No. 2 all time behind Rock.

Notre Dame has won 21 national championships, more than any other football program in the nation. Of that total, 11 were consensus selections, and eight have come in the AP era (beginning in 1936), also unmatched numbers.

Seven Heisman Trophy winners hail from Notre Dame: Angelo Bertelli in 1943, Johnny Lujack in 1947, Leon Hart in 1949, John Lattner in 1953, Paul Hornung in 1956, John Huarte in 1964 and Tim Brown in 1987. No other school can claim more. Notre Dame also leads the way with 179 first-team All-Americans through the years, including 78 consensus selections and 30 unanimous choices. There are 41 former Notre Dame players enshrined in the College Football Hall of Fame, again more than any other school, as is the total of five Hall of Fame coaches.

For all of the above reasons and more, it is understandable that Notre Dame Football is either loved or hated by college football fans nationwide, especially in those periods when the Fighting Irish are in contention for the national title. And in the first decade of the 21st century, Notre Dame appears to be reentering that stage, stealing the spotlight.

We're distilling the pageantry and drama of Notre Dame football into the pages that follow. It's a daunting task. No college football program in the country inspires the passion that Notre Dame football exacts from its fans—and its foes. Through the words and images we present here, you can get a taste of what college football's preeminent program is all about.

TRADITIONS AND PAGEANTRY

No other school in the nation can even approach the number of significant, time-honored traditions that encase the Notre Dame program. They're part of the vernacular: Touchdown Jesus, the Golden Dome, the Victory March. The sights and sounds of Game Day in South Bend create an unmatched spectacle, a glorious mix of tradition and color and pomp and pageantry. Here's a small sample of what makes Notre Dame football unique.

—— The Fighting Irish ——

During the 1800s, Notre Dame's football team bore the nickname "Catholics." Sometime during the early decades of the 20th century, the moniker "Fighting Irish" took hold, though the exact process by which this happened is shrouded in mystery. During the early 1920s, the team was known as the "Ramblers," or sometimes "Rockne's Ramblers," but the change was already in the works.

It may have been Northwestern's fans shouting "Kill the Fighting Irish!" during the matchup in 1899, or the exhortation from a Notre Dame player to his teammates—"What's wrong with you guys? You're all Irish and you're not fighting worth a lick!" during the 1909 Michigan game—or any number of other possible explanations. The roster was dominated by Irish surnames, and by the end of the Rockne regime "Ramblers" had gradually evolved into "Fighting Irish."

—— Gold and Blue —— and Sometimes Green

When Father Edward Sorin, a 28-year-old French priest of the Congregation of Holy Cross, founded the University of Notre Dame du Lac in 1842, he adopted yellow and blue as the official school colors. After the dome and statue of the Blessed Mother surmounting the Administration Building were gilded, the colors changed to Gold and Blue.

Green jerseys have been used as a psychological ploy by Notre Dame coaches since the Knute Rockne years and were a prominent feature of Frank Leahy's teams. Though the team's last four appearances in green jerseys have all ended in losses, it is not likely that we've seen the last of them. The last effort was a narrow, last-second loss to undefeated defending national champion USC in 2005 in one of the greatest games ever played.

Pep Rallies

The Friday evening pep rallies are an integral part of the Notre Dame Football tradition. Historically, the band led the student body through campus to the Field House. But growing interest in the event over the last several years prompted a move to the more spacious Joyce Center. On Sept. 5, 1997, the pep rally was held in Notre Dame Stadium, in conjunction with the expansion and rededication of the facility. Some of the recognizable people who spoke at the event included Dick Vitale, Tommy Lasorda and Regis Philbin.

Gold Dust

The gold helmets worn by the Notre Dame football players on game days are emblematic of the Golden Dome over the school's administration building. Student managers mix real gold dust into the paint that they then apply to the helmets on Friday nights before home games and Thursday nights before road games.

Campus Landmarks

Golden Dome

The University of Notre Dame du Lac was founded in 1842 by Father Edward Sorin, of the Congregation of Holy Cross, who had come over from France for just that purpose.

In 1879 a fire destroyed the Main Building. After it was rebuilt, it was topped with a dome. And the dome was gilded, not painted. Atop the dome a 19-foot tall statue of the Blessed Mother, for whom the school is named and to whom it is dedicated, was placed. The statue is illuminated at night so that it glows.

The Main Building with the Golden Dome serves as the backdrop for photographs of new alumni on graduation day and a rallying point for pregame activities during football season. It is the stepping-off point for the Band of the Fighting Irish as it leads the students into the stadium on game day.

Touchdown Jesus

The 132'-tall stone mosaic on the south side of the Hesburgh Library is visible from inside Notre Dame Stadium. It is patterned after a painting by Millard Sheet called "The Word of Life." In it, Jesus is surrounded by his apostles and others and is standing with his hands upraised. This posture of the main figure has given the world the football icon known as "Touchdown Jesus."

We're No. 1 Moses

Just outside the Hesburgh Library stands a bronze statue depicting Moses having just descended to the foot of Mount Sinai, chastising the Israelites who have taken to worshiping idols in his absence. He is cradling the stone tablets containing the Ten Commandments with his left arm and pointing to the sky with his right forefinger. Hence the nickname, "We're No. 1 Moses."

Fair Catch Corby

During the Civil War, Father William J. Corby, C.S.C., of the University of Notre Dame, served as a chaplain in the Union Army. A statue placed in front of Corby Hall depicts Father Corby with his hand raised, giving absolution to the men of the Irish Brigade as they prepare to go into action on the second day of the Battle of Gettysburg, July 2, 1863.

The raised hand suggests a punt returner signaling for a fair catch, and the piece is therefore known to students and alumni as "Fair Catch Corby."

—— Notre Dame Stadium ——

Notre Dame has been playing football in "The House that Rockne Built" for 76 years. The football team's previous home was Cartier Field, just north of the current stadium. But the old venue could hold no more than 30,000 spectators, and with coach Knute Rockne at the helm, that just wasn't enough.

Rockne himself drew up the blueprints for Notre Dame Stadium, and the new facility was dedicated on Oct. 4, 1930, with a 20–14 victory over SMU. Tragically, Rockne got to coach only one season in the new stadium before he was killed in a plane crash on March 31, 1931.

Since 1966, every game at Notre Dame but one has been a sellout. That's 209 of the last 210 home dates. The only exception was a Thanksgiving Day 1973 contest against Air Force, a scheduling accommodation for television on a holiday when the students were away from campus.

Notre Dame Stadium was expanded from the traditional 59,075 capacity to 80,232 by the start of the 1997 season. In 2001 that number was upped to the current 80,795.

When Irish Backs Go Marching By

Rah! Rah! Rah!

Up! Notre Dame men answer the cry

Gathering foemen fling to the sky

Fight! Fight! Fight!

Brave hosts advancing challenging your name

March to the battle, Notre Dame!

And when the Irish backs go marching by

The cheering thousands shout their battle cry:

For Notre Dame men are marching into the game,

Fighting the fight for you, Notre Dame.

And when the Irish line goes smashing through

They'll sweep the foemen's ranks away;

When Notre Dame men fight for Gold and Blue,

Then Notre Dame men will win the day.

The Band of the Fighting Irish

The Notre Dame marching band, officially known as the Band of the Fighting Irish, is the oldest such aggregation in existence. Founded in 1845, it is 161 years old. The band has been present at every home football game—all 385 of them—in school history.

The Band of the Fighting Irish was one of the first in the nation to include pageantry, precision drill and picture formations. In 1970 the band began to include women from Saint Mary's College before the university went co-educational in 1972.

On game day, there is the "Concert on the Steps" at Bond Hall. From there, the band marches through campus, leading the students to the stadium. The band marches into the tunnel, waits for the whistle to blow and explodes out onto the playing field for the pregame festivities.

Victory March

Rally sons of Notre Dame

Sing her glory and sound her fame

Raise her gold and blue

And cheer with voices true:

Rah, rah for Notre Dame

We will fight in every game,

Strong of heart and true to her name

We will ne'er forget her

And will cheer her ever

Loyal to Notre Dame

Cheer, cheer for old Notre Dame,

Wake up the echoes cheering her name,

Send a volley cheer on high,

Shake down the thunder from the sky.

What though the odds be great or small

Old Notre Dame will win over all,

While her loyal sons are marching

Onward to victory.

Irish Guard

The Irish Guard leads the band into the tunnel and out to the field at Notre Dame Stadium for every home game. Each member of the Guard is dressed in an Irish kilt. Including the bearskin shako atop each of their heads, they stand eight feet tall.

The guardsmen are selected on the basis of marching ability, appearance and spirit. The colors of the kilt are the "Notre Dame plaid," with the school colors of gold and blue, and the green representing the Irish.

The Notre Dame Grotto

Alma Mater
(Notre Dame, Our Mother)

Notre Dame, our mother

Tender, strong and true

Proudly in the heavens,

Gleams thy gold and blue.

Glory's mantle cloaks thee

Golden is thy fame,

And our hearts forever,

Praise thee, Notre Dame.

And our hearts forever,

Love thee, Notre Dame.

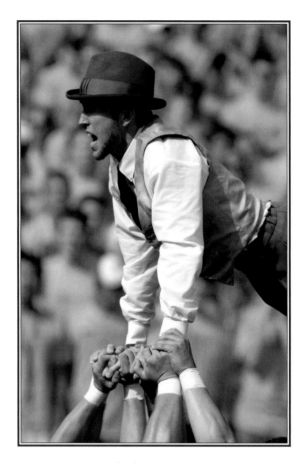

Mascots

From the 1930s through the 1950s, the mascot of the Fighting Irish was a succession of Irish Terriers. The first, named Brick Top Shaun Rhu, was donated to Knute Rockne in 1930 by Cleveland native Charles Otis. Through the years, most of the terrier mascots bore the name Clashmore Mike. In 1965, the leprechaun replaced Clashmore Mike as the school's official mascot. The leprechaun is consistent with the Notre Dame nickname and is now an integral part of the game-day atmosphere.

"Moose"

Edward "Moose" Krause served as Notre Dame's athletic director for more than 30 years, from 1949–1981. Before graduating from Notre Dame in 1934, he had become an All-American in both football and basketball. He was Notre Dame's head basketball coach from 1942–1947, leading the Irish to a 98–48 record.

During his time as athletic director, Notre Dame's football team won four consensus national championships. On Sept. 17, 1999, the day before that year's Notre Dame–Michigan State game, a bronze sculpture of Moose was dedicated in front of the Joyce Center. He sits on a bench looking toward Notre Dame Stadium.

Movies

Knute Rockne, All-American

In 1940 *Knute Rockne, All-American* debuted in theaters across the country. The film starred Pat O'Brien as the legendary coach and future U.S. president Ronald Reagan as George Gipp. In 1997, the Library of Congress designated *Knute Rockne, All-American* as a part of the National Film Registry, qualifying it as an "irreplaceable part of America's cinematic heritage."

Rudy

Rudy, a movie telling the story of Dan "Rudy" Ruettiger, was released in 1993. Rudy, a walk-on football player during the Ara Parseghian and Dan Devine coaching tenures, played 27 seconds in the 1975 Georgia Tech game, the last game of his senior year, after two years of sacrifice helping to prepare the team for each game.

Ronald Reagan as the Gipper in Knute Rockne, All-American.

——— Shillelagh ———

The USC–Notre Dame series is the greatest and most storied intersectional rivalry in all of sports. Each year a trophy is awarded to the winner—a jeweled shillelagh. A shillelagh is a Gaelic war club made of either oak or blackthorn saplings, purportedly because they are the only things tougher than an Irish skull. The foot-long shillelagh has ruby-adorned Trojan heads with the year and score of the SC wins, while emerald-studded shamrocks represent Notre Dame wins. According to legend, the original shillelagh was flown from Ireland by Howard Hughes' pilot, and was first presented in 1952 by the Notre Dame Club of Los Angeles. The rivals are currently on their second shillelagh, the first one having been retired and put on display permanently at Notre Dame.

Actually, there are two shillelagh trophies in Notre Dame football tradition. The second has passed back and forth to the winner of the Notre Dame–Purdue game since 1957. It was donated by the late Joe McLaughlin, a merchant seaman and Notre Dame fan who brought the club back from Ireland. Following each contest between the two teams, a football with the winner's initial and the final score is attached to the stand.

Angelo Bertelli

THE GREATEST PLAYERS

Notre Dame's roster of greats reads like a who's who of college football legends. The names are familiar to fans of college football, and for the fans of the Fighting Irish's rivals, they still bring a shiver of dread. Here are some of the stars who have shone brightest during their tenures in South Bend.

Notre Dame has had so many national award winners, so many great players, that they can't all be included here, which is why the following list should be considered representative, not definitive. We start with the players who have bestowed the nickname "Heisman U" on Notre Dame.

"Heisman U"

ANGELO BERTELLI
Quarterback
1943 Heisman Trophy

Angelo Bertelli, a.k.a. the Springfield Rifle, was inducted into the College Football Hall of Fame in 1972, 30 years after he eased Notre Dame's transition from the single wing to the T-formation under Frank Leahy. In 1941, Leahy's first year as head coach at his alma mater, Bertelli threw for more than 1,000 yards as a single-wing tailback and led the Irish to an 8–0–1 record and third-place final national ranking. He finished second to Minnesota's Bruce Smith in the Heisman voting that fall, and sixth in 1942 after transforming into a T-formation quarterback. As a senior in 1943, with America embroiled in World War II, Bertelli answered the call of the Marine Corps and reported for service after six games. Before leaving the team, Bertelli had completed 69 percent of his passes, throwing for 10 scores. He sparked the Irish to a 6–0 record and 43.5 points per game, propelling the team to the national championship. He was awarded the Heisman Trophy while he was in boot camp.

JOHNNY LUJACK
Quarterback
1947 Heisman Trophy

Lujack, a 1960 Hall of Fame inductee, took over as Notre Dame's quarterback six games into the 1943 season, when Angelo Bertelli left to join the Marines. In his first collegiate start, versus Army in 1943, Lujack threw for two touchdowns, ran for another and intercepted a pass. He spent the next two years in the Navy, returning to Notre Dame after World War II ended. He was one of the keys to establishing the school's total dominance of the game in the postwar years of 1946–1949. With Lujack as the starting quarterback in 1946 and 1947, the Fighting Irish won two national titles and never lost a game. There was the memorable scoreless tie with Army in 1946 in which Lujack, playing safety, saved the Irish from defeat with an open-field tackle of Army fullback Doc Blanchard, the reigning Heisman winner. They played both ways in those days, and many believed Lujack was even better on defense than offense. The 1947 Notre Dame team is arguably the greatest in college football history, with Lujack as its Heisman-winning quarterback. As a pro with the Chicago Bears for four years, Lujack threw for 468 yards in one game, intercepted a record eight passes on defense as a rookie and led the team in scoring all four years.

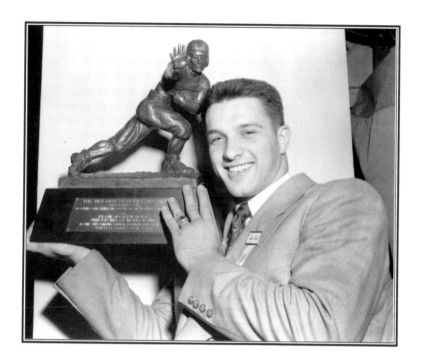

LEON HART
End
1949 Heisman Trophy

Only two linemen ever won the Heisman Trophy—Yale's Larry Kelley in 1936 and Notre Dame's Leon Hart in 1949. With Hart starting at right end for four years from 1946 to 1949, Notre Dame never lost a game. With college football teams nationwide adopting the two-platoon system, Hart was one of the last of the game's iron men. He was equally devastating to opponents on both sides of the ball. A three-year first-team All-American and two-time consensus pick, Hart made his name as a pass receiver—more than one-fourth of his catches went for touchdowns—but he was also devastating as a blocker, tackler and pass rusher. His 1949 honors included both the Heisman Trophy and the Maxwell Award as the nation's best player. Over his eight-year career with the Detroit Lions, Hart helped the team to three NFL titles and was an All-Pro on both offense and defense in 1951. He was enshrined in the College Football Hall of Fame in 1973.

JOHN LATTNER

Halfback

1953 Heisman Trophy

Lattner won the Heisman as a senior in 1953, Frank Leahy's last season as Notre Dame's coach. That year the Fighting Irish went 9–0–1 and finished second in the final wire service polls. Lattner had finished fifth in Heisman voting as a junior and won the Maxwell Award as the nation's top player both seasons. Over his three-year career, Lattner averaged 4.9 yards per carry with 20 rushing touchdowns and intercepted 13 passes. His school record for all-purpose yards (rushing, receiving and returns) stood for more than a quarter century. As a senior he averaged more than 40 yards on eight kickoff returns, running two back for touchdowns.

PAUL HORNUNG
Quarterback
1956 Heisman Trophy

In 1956 Notre Dame finished 2–8, and Paul Hornung became the first and only player to win the Heisman Trophy while playing for a losing team. As a junior in 1955, when Notre Dame went 8–2, Hornung came in fifth in Heisman voting after finishing fourth nationally in total offense with 1,215 yards. He accounted for 354 yards, the highest single-game total in the nation that year, against USC. He ran for a touchdown, threw for another and intercepted two passes in the win against fourth-ranked Navy, and he kicked the winning field goal with the clock winding down against Iowa. As a senior in 1956, he led the Irish in rushing, passing, punting, kicking and kick returns; finished second in tackles and interceptions; and scored more than half of the team's points. He accumulated 1,337 yards of total offense, second-most in the nation. As a member of the Green Bay Packers, Hornung led the NFL in scoring three straight years—1959, 1960, 1961. He is a member of both the College and Pro Football Halls of Fame.

JOHN HUARTE
Quarterback
1964 Heisman Trophy

After a disastrous 2–7 campaign in 1963, Notre Dame hired Ara Parseghian as coach and the Irish stormed to nine straight wins in 1964 before falling in the last minute and a half at USC to go 9–1. The quarterback of that Fighting Irish offense was senior John Huarte, who had been little-used in his previous varsity seasons. In 1964, Ara's debut season, Huarte teamed with receiver Jack Snow to form the nation's deadliest pass-catch duo. Huarte opened the season with 270 yards passing, including touchdown throws of 61 and 42 yards to Snow, in an upset win over Wisconsin. For the year he completed 56 percent of his passes for 2,062 yards and 16 touchdowns, ranked third nationally in total offense with 2,069 yards and collected Notre Dame's sixth Heisman Trophy.

TIM BROWN
Flanker
1987 Heisman Trophy

After a sensational junior campaign in 1986, Tim Brown won Notre Dame's seventh Heisman Trophy as a senior in 1987. Brown finished his junior year with a 254-total-yard performance in the 38–37 come-from-behind upset of USC, with a 56-yard punt return to set up the winning field goal. He nailed down the award when he returned back-to-back punts for touchdowns in the 1987 Michigan State game. As a junior he finished third nationally in all-purpose yardage and averaged 20 yards per catch. He averaged 22 yards per reception as a senior. For his career he caught 12 touchdown passes, ran for four touchdowns, scored three times on kickoff returns and three more on punt returns. He also left Notre Dame as the school's all-time leader in receiving yardage (2,493). The sixth overall pick in the 1988 NFL Draft, Brown was a nine-time Pro Bowler during his career with the Raiders.

———— The Legend of George Gipp ————

George Gipp might have been the most electrifying football player of all time. His school career rushing record was not broken for 58 years, and on defense he never allowed a pass completion in his area—not one in four years.

Gipp went to Notre Dame in 1916 on a baseball scholarship, but coach Knute Rockne, an assistant at the time under Jesse Harper, spotted him playing around on the practice field in early September, in street clothes. The tall, lanky youngster was dropkicking the ball fifty yards and more with perfect ease, and Rock challenged the freshman to join the football team.

Gipp, who hailed from Laurium, Michigan, was the most versatile player of Rockne's coaching regime—running, passing, punting, kicking and returning punts and kicks. He led the team in both rushing and passing in 1918, 1919 and 1920. As a senior he ran for 827 yards at 8.1 per carry with eight touchdowns, and completed 30 of 62 passes for 709 yards and three more scores. For his career he ran for 2,341 yards, averaging 6.3 per rush with 21 touchdowns. He passed for 1,769 yards and eight TDs and intercepted five passes. And the Irish were undefeated in Gipp's last 20 games.

Gipp contracted strep throat while playing in the Northwestern game on Nov. 20, 1920, and died of complications on Dec. 14 after a record-setting All-America career. On his deathbed (so the story goes), Gipp asked his coach to have a Notre Dame team "win one for the Gipper" some day.

Rockne agreed and fulfilled his promise on November 10, 1928. That injury-decimated Irish squad, which eventually finished the season 5–4 (as close to a losing record as Rockne would come) faced a powerful Army team.

In the locker room before the game, Rockne drew his players around him, waited for the room to fall silent, and repeated Gipp's dying words: "I've got to go, Rock. It's all right. I'm not afraid. Some time, Rock, when the team is up against it, when things are wrong and the breaks are beating the boys, tell them to go in there with all they've got and win just one for the Gipper. I don't know where I'll be then, Rock. But I'll know about it, and I'll be happy." With his players choked with emotion, Rockne continued: "This is the day, and you are the team."

The doors nearly flew off their hinges as the team stormed out to the field. The Irish won 12–6 on a one-yard touchdown run by Jack Chevigny ("That's one for the Gipper," he shouted from the end zone) and a 32-yard Butch Niemiec–to–Johnny O'Brien touchdown pass.

The Four Horsemen of Notre Dame

The Notre Dame–Army series is no longer a part of the college football landscape, but while it was, it saw some of the most history-making games in the sport's history. There was the Dorais-to-Rockne game of 1913; the "Win one for the Gipper" game of 1928; and in between the two came perhaps the best-known one of all. Here's Grantland Rice's legendary lead in the *New York Herald Tribune* describing the Notre Dame–Army game played on October 18, 1924:

"Outlined against a blue-gray October sky the four horsemen rode again. In dramatic lore they are known as famine, pestilence, destruction and death. These are only aliases. Their real names are Stuhldreher, Miller, Crowley and Layden. They formed the crest of the South Bend cyclone before which another fighting Army football team was swept over the precipice at the Polo Grounds yesterday afternoon as 55,000 spectators peered down on the bewildering panorama spread on the green plain below."

Thanks to Rice, the Notre Dame backfield of quarterback Harry Stuhldreher, left halfback Jim Crowley, right halfback Don Miller and fullback Elmer Layden will live forever as the Four Horsemen of Notre Dame.

It didn't hurt that Knute Rockne was their coach. Or that a student publicity aide named George Strickler, after reading Rice's piece, had them photographed in their uniforms astride horses from the livery stable in town. Or that they played behind a great line known as the Seven Mules, featuring Hall of Famers Adam Walsh at center and Rip Miller at tackle.

Miller, Crowley and Layden combined for more than 5,000 rushing yards and 42 touchdown runs over their career, while Stuhldreher was a cocky, fearless field general. He was deadly accurate as a passer, intercepted three passes as a junior and ran back a punt for a touchdown.

Inspired by Grantland Rice's immortal article, Notre Dame student publicity aide George Strickler cemented the legend of the Four Horsemen with this impromptu photograph.

Other than the Army game, the Irish were never threatened with a loss during that 1924 season. They finished the regular season 9–0, then beat an undefeated Stanford 11 starring All-America fullback Ernie Nevers and coached by Glenn "Pop" Warner. Layden scored three times, including two on interception returns of 78 and 70 yards, for a 27–10 victory, a 10–0 record and Notre Dame's first consensus national title.

All four players are enshrined in the College Football Hall of Fame, with Layden a charter member (elected in 1951).

—— Joe Cool ——

"Joe was born to be a quarterback." These are the words of Joe Montana's high school coach, Jeff Petrucci. Montana wasn't particularly tall, certainly wasn't fast and didn't have a particularly strong arm. Yet he is commonly referred to as the greatest quarterback of all time.

Frank Carideo (1928–1930) and Johnny Lujack (1943, 1946–1947), who played for Rockne and Leahy, respectively, are known to college football historians as the best quarterbacks who ever took the field for Notre Dame. Both were two-year unanimous All-Americans. Lujack won a Heisman (Carideo would have, had the award been in existence during his day), and both quarterbacked the Irish to back-to-back national titles. Montana didn't win a Heisman and he didn't make All-America, though he did win a national title as a junior in 1977. But after his NFL career with the San Francisco 49ers, he is certainly the popular choice among today's fans who remember him as the best quarterback they ever saw play.

At Notre Dame, Montana was the Comeback Kid. He started three games as a sophomore in 1975 for first-year Irish coach Dan Devine, then missed the 1976 season with an injury. When the 1977 season opened, he was No. 3 on the depth chart, and the Irish were already 1–1 before Devine inserted him into a game. The Irish were trailing Purdue 24–14 when Montana came off the bench with 11 minutes remaining in the game and led the Irish to 17 points, throwing for 154 yards in the 31–24 win.

What Montana pulled off in the 1979 Cotton Bowl, a.k.a. the Chicken Soup Game, against Houston was truly a miracle. It was also the greatest comeback win in Notre Dame history. The game was played in an ice storm, and Montana missed most of the third quarter with hypothermia. He was administered a dose of chicken soup to bring his body temperature up to normal. The Irish trailed the Cougars 34–12 midway through the fourth quarter when the Irish rallied for 23 points. Montana ran for a touchdown, threw for another and also connected on a pair of two-point conversion passes, including one with no time left on the clock, for the 35–34 victory in the last game of his college career.

But what most casual fans remember are his years as a pro, when he piloted the 49ers to four Super Bowl titles. Joe Cool, as Montana became known, is still the only player in NFL history to win three Super Bowl MVP awards.

"The first dream in my life was to go to Notre Dame."
—JOE MONTANA

Fighting Irish Players ——— in the College Football Hall of Fame

The players on the following pages have been honored with induction into the College Football Hall of Fame, which, appropriately enough, now resides in South Bend, Indiana.

ANGELO BERTELLI
Quarterback, 1941–1943
Inducted 1972

JIM CROWLEY
Halfback, 1922–1924
Inducted 1966

GEORGE GIPP
Halfback, 1917–1920
Inducted 1951

LEON HART
End, 1946–1949
Inducted 1973

PAUL HORNUNG
Quarterback, 1954–1956
Inducted 1985

JOHN HUARTE
Quarterback, 1961–1964
Inducted 2005

JOHN LATTNER
Halfback, 1951–1953
Inducted 1979

ELMER LAYDEN
Fullback, 1922–1924
Inducted 1951

DON MILLER
Halfback, 1922–1924
Inducted 1970

JOHNNY LUJACK
Quarterback, 1943, 1946–1947
Inducted 1960

HARRY STUHLDREHER
Quarterback, 1922–1924
Inducted 1958

Please see player biographies on pages 22–35

HEARTLEY "HUNK" ANDERSON
Guard, 1918–1921
Inducted 1974

Many people know Anderson succeeded Knute Rockne as Notre Dame's coach, but most don't realize he was a first-team All-America guard in 1921 while playing for Rockne. Anderson was a four-year starter, playing on Rockne's first team in 1918, and blocking for George Gipp for three years (1918–1920). The Irish were 31–2–2 during Anderson's playing days.

College Football Hall of Fame

ROSS BROWNER
Defensive End, 1973, 1975–1977
Inducted 1999

Browner was a four-year starter who played for two Notre Dame national champion squads, as a freshman in 1973 and as a senior in 1977. He was a two-time consensus All-American, in 1976 and 1977. He won the Outland Trophy in 1976 and the Lombardi in 1977, when he finished seventh in the Heisman voting. He still holds Notre Dame career records for tackles for losses in a single season (28 in 1976) and career (77), and for career fumble recoveries (12). He also blocked two kicks and scored two safeties and one touchdown.

JACK CANNON
Guard, 1927–1929
Inducted 1965

Cannon was a consensus All-America guard for Knute Rockne's 1929 national champions. In the 1929 win over Army at Yankee Stadium, Cannon threw the key block for Jack Elder, who ran 96 yards for the winning touchdown. In 1947, famed sportswriter Grantland Rice declared Cannon the greatest guard in Notre Dame history.

FRANK CARIDEO
Quarterback, 1928–1930
Inducted 1954

Carideo is arguably the greatest quarterback in Notre Dame history. He certainly was Knute Rockne's greatest quarterback, and he was the field general for what Rock believed to be his best team, the 1930 national champions. Carideo was a starter for two seasons, 1929–1930, winning two national championships. He was a consensus All-American both years, and he won every game he started.

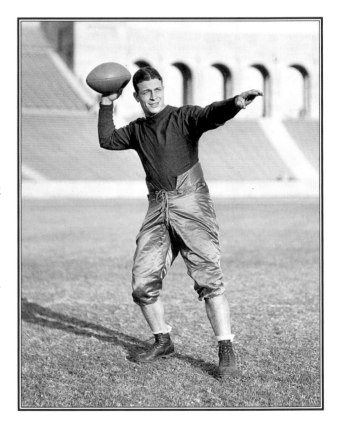

Already in his hoops gear prior to the start of a Notre Dame basketball game, Irish All-American football star George Connor (left) is presented with a postseason award from Francis Powers, president of the Football Writers Association of America, after the 1947 campaign.

GEORGE CONNOR
Tackle, 1946–1947
Inducted 1963

Connor won the inaugural Outland Trophy in 1946 for coach Frank Leahy's national champions. He was captain of the legendary 1947 team and was a consensus All-American both years he played. Notre Dame never lost a game during Connor's playing days and was national champion both years.

★★★★★

ZYGMONT "ZIGGY" CZAROBSKI
Tackle, 1942–1943, 1946–1947
Inducted 1977

Czarobski joined fellow Irish tackle starter George Connor as a first-team All-American in 1947. He started for coach Frank Leahy's national champions in 1943, then spent two years in the military during World War II. He returned after the war to start at right tackle on the great 1946 and 1947 national title teams.

BOB DOVE
End, 1940–1942
Inducted 2000

Dove was a two-year consensus All-American on coach Frank Leahy's first two Irish squads, in 1941 and 1942. In 1939, Dove caught 15 passes for 187 yards from future Heisman Trophy winner Angelo Bertelli. In 1942, Dove won the Rockne Trophy (precursor to the Outland Trophy, including ends) as the nation's outstanding college lineman.

RAY EICHENLAUB
Fullback, 1911–1914
Inducted 1972

Gus Dorais and Knute Rockne weren't the only All-Americans on coach Jesse Harper's 1913 Notre Dame team. They were joined by bruising fullback Ray "Iron Eich" Eichenlaub. He was a four-year starter. He scored 12 touchdowns as a senior and finished with 176 career points. He was also a four-year letterman in track.

Bill "Moose" Fischer (left), was the winner of the Outland Trophy as the nation's top lineman.

BILL "MOOSE" FISCHER
Guard, 1945–1948
Inducted 1983

Fischer was a consensus All-American in both his junior and senior years, 1947 and 1948. He was a three-year starter and captain of the 1948 national champions. Also in 1948, he became the second Notre Dame player to win the Outland Trophy in three years (along with George Connor in 1946).

JERRY GROOM
Center/Linebacker, 1948–1950
Inducted 1994

Groom was a consensus All-American with the 1950 Irish team, of which he served as captain. He started both ways, at center and linebacker, his junior and senior years, and he was a key component of the 1949 national title team. Over his three-year career, he played 465 minutes—86 percent of the total possible time.

RALPH GUGLIELMI
Quarterback, 1951–1954
Inducted 2001

Guglielmi was a three-year starter and was a unanimous All-American as a senior. He completed 208 of 435 career pass attempts for 3,073 yards and 18 touchdowns, ran for 12 more scores, intercepted 10 passes and ran one back for a score, recovered two fumbles and kicked five extra points. He finished fourth in the Heisman Trophy voting in 1954.

FRANK "NORDY" HOFFMAN
Guard, 1930–1931
Inducted 1978

Hoffman was a first-team All-American as a senior in 1931, while playing next to a fellow Hall of Famer, center Tommy Yarr. Hoffman led the 1931 Irish in interceptions with three.

JIM LYNCH
Linebacker, 1964–1966
Inducted 1992

Lynch was captain of the 1966 Fighting Irish team that won the national championship. He was a unanimous first-team All-American that season and also the recipient of the Maxwell Award as the nation's outstanding college football player.

KEN MACAFEE
Tight End, 1974–1977
Inducted 1997

MacAfee was a three-time first-team All-American, from 1975 to 1977. He was a unanimous pick in his senior year of 1977, when he finished third in Heisman Trophy voting and became the first lineman to win the Walter Camp Player of the Year award. Also in that national championship season of 1977, MacAfee caught 54 passes from his tight end spot for 797 yards and six touchdowns. For his career, he caught 128 passes for 1,759 yards and 15 touchdowns. And he was a devastating blocker.

JIM MARTIN
End/Tackle, 1946–1949
Inducted 1995

Martin started for four years during the late 1940s, when the Fighting Irish did not lose a game and won three of the four national titles. Martin played both ways, his first three years at end and at tackle as a senior. He was co-captain of the 1949 national champions, and he led that squad in minutes played with 405.

BERT METZGER
Guard, 1928–1930
Inducted 1982

A 5'9", 149-pound guard on Rockne's last two teams, in 1929 and 1930, Metzger was the spearhead of the line. Those two teams were unbeaten, untied and national champions both years and outscored their opposition 410–112 with Metzger at right guard. He was a first-team All-American as a senior in 1930.

CREIGHTON MILLER
Halfback, 1941–1943
Inducted 1976

A nephew of Four Horseman Don Miller, Creighton Miller is the only Notre Dame player to lead the nation in rushing for a season. In 1943, Miller topped the national charts with 911 rushing yards, the second-highest single-season total in school history to that time, and ran for 13 touchdowns for the national champions. He was also a consensus All-American that season, when he finished fourth in Heisman Trophy voting. Incidentally, Irish quarterback Angelo Bertelli won the Heisman that year.

EDGAR "RIP" MILLER
Tackle, 1922–1924
Inducted 1966

Miller was one of the famous Seven Mules— the line that cleared the way for the Four Horsemen. Over three years with Miller at right tackle, the Irish went 27–2–1, including 10–0 in 1924, when the Irish won their first consensus national championship.

FRED MILLER
Tackle, 1926–1928
Inducted 1985

Miller was a three-year starter at left tackle for Knute Rockne's Fighting Irish. He was a first-team All-American in 1928 before graduating cum laude, with the highest academic average among the monogram athletes at Notre Dame.

WAYNE MILLNER
End, 1933–1935
Inducted 1990

Millner caught the winning touchdown pass with less than two minutes remaining in the 1935 Ohio State game, which is widely recognized as the greatest football game ever played. He was a three-year starter at left end and a consensus All-American as a senior.

ALAN PAGE
Defensive End, 1964–1966
Inducted 1993

Page made 63 tackles for the great 1966 Irish team that won the national title. He was a three-year starter at defensive right end and a consensus All-American as a senior. He posted 134 career tackles, recovered four fumbles, broke up two passes and scored one touchdown.

LOUIS "RED" SALMON
Fullback, 1900–1903
Inducted 1971

Salmon was Notre Dame's first All-American. His single-season scoring record of 105 points in 1903 and his 36 career touchdowns were school records that stood until 1984. He scored 250 career points, a school record that stood until 1985, even though touchdowns counted for only five points when he played.

MARCHY SCHWARTZ
Halfback, 1929–1931
Inducted 1974

Schwartz was a consensus All-American in 1930 and was a unanimous pick as a senior in 1931. He led the team in rushing, passing and scoring for both his junior and senior seasons. He was a key component of the 1930 national title run in Rockne's final season at the helm. He ranked second to George Gipp in career rushing and still stands 10th in school history with 1,945 career yards at 5.5 per carry.

BILL SHAKESPEARE
Halfback, 1933–1935
Inducted 1983

Known as the Bard of Staten Island, Shakespeare started at left halfback for coach Elmer Layden in 1934 and 1935 and was a first-team All-American as a senior. He is best known for throwing the winning touchdown pass to Wayne Millner in the epic battle with Ohio State in 1935. He stood as Notre Dame's career punting leader for more than a half-century.

EMIL SITKO
Halfback/Fullback, 1946–1949
Inducted 1984

The media referred to him as "Six-yard" Sitko; his friends and schoolmates knew him as Red. He was a two-time consensus All-American and a unanimous pick for the 1949 national champions. During the four years Sitko played for coach Frank Leahy, the Fighting Irish never lost a game. He ran for 2,226 yards and 26 touchdowns over his career, averaging 6.1 yards per carry. He averaged 7.1 yards per carry with the immortal 1947 squad.

★★★★★

JOE THEISMANN
Quarterback, 1968–1970
Inducted 2003

Theismann was a first-team All-American and runner-up to Stanford's Jim Plunkett in the Heisman derby of 1970. He was voted team MVP that year after quarterbacking the Irish to a 10–0 record and a 24–11 victory over top-ranked Texas in the Cotton Bowl.

JOHN "CLIPPER" SMITH
Guard, 1925–1927
Inducted 1975

Smith bounced around between fullback, halfback and center before settling in at guard, where he was a starter as a junior and senior. He was consensus All-American in 1927, when he served as team captain.

★★★★★

46

ADAM WALSH
Center, 1922–1924
Inducted 1968

Walsh was captain of Notre Dame's 1924 national title team, spearheading the line known as the Seven Mules. He was a two-year starting center, blocking for the Four Horsemen in 1923 and 1924. Walsh played the Army game in 1924 with two broken hands, intercepting a pass and leading the team in tackles.

★★★★★

BOB WILLIAMS
Quarterback, 1948–1950
Inducted 1988

Williams' single-season 161.4 passing efficiency rating in 1949 still ranks as the best in Notre Dame history. He was a consensus All-American that fall, finishing fifth in the Heisman voting and sixth as a senior the following year, 1950.

★★★★★

TOMMY YARR
Center, 1929–1931
Inducted 1987

Yarr was the starting center on the team Knute Rockne believed to be his best, in 1930. In the SMU game that year, Yarr intercepted two passes in the game's closing minutes to ensure the win. In 1931, he was team captain and a consensus All-American.

More Great Players

RAGHIB "ROCKET" ISMAIL
Flanker, 1988–1990

The Rocket might be the fastest player in the history of college football. And he wasn't a track star who played football on the side; he was a football player who happened to have unbelievable speed. He helped the Irish to a national title as a freshman in 1988, and he was a two-time consensus All-American in 1989 and 1990. He finished second in the 1990 Heisman race and won the Walter Camp Player of the Year Award that same year. He holds Notre Dame career records with 22.0 yards per pass reception and five kickoff returns for touchdowns. He ran back two kickoffs for touchdowns in a single game twice—against Rice in 1988 and Michigan in 1989.

"He's one of the greatest nose guards we've played against."
—PENN STATE COACH JOE PATERNO ON CHRIS ZORICH

CHRIS ZORICH
Nose Tackle, 1988–1990

As a sophomore in 1988, Zorich started at nose tackle for coach Lou Holtz's national champion Fighting Irish. As a senior in 1990, he was a unanimous first-team All-America selection and Lombardi Award winner as the nation's best lineman. Over his three-year career, Zorich collected 219 tackles, including 21 behind the line.

HARPER AT NOTRE DAME 34-5-1	
YEAR	RECORD
1913	7–0
1914	6–2
1915	7–1
1916	8–1
1917	6–1–1

THE COACHES

It has taken the leadership of great men to produce the legacy and tradition that embody Notre Dame football. Many Irish coaches stand among the greats the game has produced, including possibly the greatest coach in football history.

Jesse Harper
1913-1917

Contrary to popular misconception, Notre Dame football was not an unknown quantity until Knute Rockne's reign as coach. Rockne played end at Notre Dame, and the school made a huge splash in the football waters in Rock's senior year, 1913, the first year of Jesse Harper's tenure as coach. That was the year quarterback Gus Dorais and his roommate, Rockne, teamed up to shock mighty Army 35–13 on the Plain at West Point.

The Irish finished that season undefeated. In five years at Notre Dame, Harper's teams lost only five games.

Harper played football under the immortal Amos Alonzo Stagg at the University of Chicago, a national powerhouse on the gridiron in those days. He enjoyed successful coaching stints at Alma College in Michigan and Wabash College in Indiana before taking the Notre Dame job. He retired from coaching in 1917 at the age of 33. In 1971, he was elected to the College Football Hall of Fame.

——— Knute Rockne ———
1918-1930

Notre Dame's Knute Rockne is the greatest football coach in history. Period. He seized the public's imagination and single-handedly popularized the game of football nationwide. From coast to coast, fans adored him.

Rockne's teams won with deception, finesse and lightning speed, inspiring spectators and opponents. On average, his teams outscored their opponents by more than four to one. During Rockne's tenure in South Bend, attendance figures across the nation began to skyrocket, and at Notre Dame games they multiplied almost tenfold.

Rockne was born on March 4, 1888, in Voss, Norway, and immigrated to the United States with his family when he was five. The Rocknes settled in Chicago, and legend has it that young Knute fell in love with the game of American football while watching the great Walter Eckersall play in high school.

As a Notre Dame player from 1910 to 1913, Rockne was instrumental in thrusting his school into the nation's football consciousness. By the end of his all-too-brief coaching career from 1918 to 1930, he had led the Notre Dame football program into elite status and beyond. In his early years at the helm, Rockne took his underdog Ramblers on the road and consistently beat the best the game had to offer.

The anybody, anywhere, anytime character of Rockne's early teams inspired the phenomenon known as the "subway alumni"—people who never went to college but could identify with an underdog winning against all odds. By the end of his reign, Rockne's Ramblers (a nickname with which Rock himself was not particularly enamored) were no longer underdogs, and they had become known as the Fighting Irish.

While watching the performance of a chorus line, Rockne conceived the idea of what came to be known as the Notre Dame Shift. The backs would line up in a T-formation, then

shift rapidly into a single wing (Rockne's version was called the "box" formation), with all four backs in motion at the snap, before the defense could get set. No other team could duplicate it with the required precision, and no defense could handle it. The Notre Dame Shift is the reason the rules now require a full-second stop after a shift and prohibit more than one man in motion when the ball is snapped.

During that time, substitutions were strictly limited, precluding the use of two platoons. So Rockne employed what he called his "shock troops," an entire team of backups who started games and wore down their opponents before giving way to the real first string.

Rockne played end for Notre Dame under coaches Frank Longman, John Marks and Jesse Harper. During Harper's first year at the helm (1913), Rockne teamed with his roommate, quarterback Gus Dorais, as the pass-catch combo that shook the college football world to its foundation.

Rockne and Dorais worked as janitors and busboys at a beachfront hotel in Cedar Point, Ohio, in the summer of 1913, and during their off hours they worked at an athletic field near the hotel perfecting a weapon that had been legalized in 1906—the forward pass. They led their team from its obscure, unknown school in northern Indiana to the Plain at West Point on November 1 to take what was expected to be a shellacking at the hands of mighty Army. Then they unleashed their attack.

Before that day, a receiver would run a designated distance downfield, turn to face his quarterback, wait for the ball to come to him and cradle it away in his breadbasket with his arms. Beginning that day with Dorais and Rockne, the receiver would run established pass routes and timing patterns. The quarterback would lead the receiver, who caught the ball on the run with his hands. The world was not ready for this. Dorais completed an unheard-of 14 of 17 for 243 yards in that historic game, and his 40-yard completion to Rockne was the longest pass play at that time. Notre Dame stunned the Cadets 35–13 and sent a shock wave through the football world. The forward pass was on its way to becoming a major part of the game, and Notre Dame was a household name.

Rockne worked his way through school, was a star in track as well as football, and graduated magna cum laude. He accepted a graduate assistantship in chemistry while also serving as an assistant on Harper's coaching staff. He was named head coach upon Harper's resignation in early 1918.

In his 13 seasons as Notre Dame's coach, Rockne compiled a record of 105–12–5, with six perfect seasons and five national titles. Three of them (in 1924, 1929 and 1930) were consensus selections. His winning percentage of .881 is the highest in history, college or pro. He is the only coach ever who coached 10 years or more and had fewer career losses than seasons coached.

Rockne produced 20 first-team All-Americans, including some of the game's most legendary figures. The Four Horsemen and the Seven Mules finished the 1924 season 10–0 and captured the national title. They concluded the campaign as 27–10 Rose Bowl victors over an undefeated Stanford 11 led by All-America fullback Ernie Nevers and coached by Glenn "Pop" Warner.

George Gipp, one of the greatest football players who ever lived, was another of Rockne's immortals. Gipp's school career record of 2,341 rushing yards from 1917 to 1920

stood for more than a half century, and the Irish were undefeated in his last 20 games.

Gipp can realistically be credited with a historic win eight years after he died of strep throat on Dec. 14, 1920, with Rockne at his bedside. On Nov. 10, 1928, against Army, Rockne exhorted his outmanned troops to win one for the Gipper. Fulfilling Gipp's dying request, the Irish won 12–6. The Irish finished the campaign at 5–4, and a loss to Army that day would have hung Rockne with the only losing record of his career.

Rockne's last two teams, in 1929 and 1930, were his best. They were quarterbacked by Frank Carideo, whose name may be unfamiliar to most fans today but who might have been Notre Dame's greatest quarterback ever. He was a consensus All-American both seasons and won every game he started. In 1929, with Notre Dame Stadium under construction, Rockne's Ramblers played the entire schedule away from home and finished a perfect 9–0. The 13–12 win over USC that season was played in front of a crowd of approximately 120,000 at Chicago's Soldier Field. Rock's 10–0 team in 1930 was his last.

On March 31, 1931, Rockne boarded Transcontinental-Western Flight 599 in Kansas City bound for Los Angeles, where he was scheduled to film a football demonstration movie. A friend, playwright Albert C. Fuller, was there to see him off. "Happy landing, Rock!" Fuller said as he waved good-bye. "Thanks, Al," Rockne said, "but I'd prefer just an ordinary soft landing." Just after takeoff, the plane encountered a storm, iced over and crashed into a wheat field near Bazaar, Kansas. All aboard the craft perished. Rockne was 43.

Foreign dignitaries, including the king of Norway, attended Rockne's funeral at the Cathedral of the Sacred Heart on the Notre Dame campus. President Herbert Hoover declared Rockne's death "a national loss." Thousands of mourners were turned away, unable to fit inside. More than one hundred thousand lined the procession route from Rockne's house on Wayne Street to the Cathedral.

ROCKNE AT NOTRE DAME 105-12-5		
YEAR	RECORD	BOWL
1913	7–0	
1918	3–1–2#	
1919*	9–0	
1920*	9–0	
1921	10–1	
1922	8–1–1	
1923	9–1	
1924**	10–0	Rose
1925	7–2–1	
1926	9–1	
1927	7–1–1	
1928	5–4	
1929**	9–0	
1930**	10–0	

#season abbreviated due to influenza epidemic

*national champions

**consensus national champions

Many years later, Elmer Layden, the fullback of the Four Horsemen backfield, remembered the shock surrounding his coach's passing: "It was almost the size of President Kennedy's impact. It was amazing. They turned out on the train, and at the funeral. He was a national hero."

During his time as football coach, Rockne also served as Notre Dame's athletic director, track coach, ticket distributor and equipment manager. He was a published author with three books to his credit, and he designed Notre Dame Stadium. It's called the House That Rock Built for a reason. Rockne is a charter member (1951) of the College Football Hall of Fame.

—— Frank Leahy ——
1941-1943, 1946-1953

He was known as the Master. Frank Leahy's winning percentage of .855 at Notre Dame ranks second only to Rockne's in Division I-A history. Add his two years as head man at Boston College in 1939 and 1940, and his career percentage shoots to .864. Rockne is the only coach of 10 or more years with fewer losses than seasons coached; Leahy is the only other, not just at Notre Dame but anywhere, whose losses did not exceed his years (11 losses in 11 seasons at ND; 13 losses in 13 seasons total).

Leahy played tackle for Rockne in 1928–1929 but missed his senior season (1930) due to injuries. Following his graduation, he embarked on a career as a line coach, first at Georgetown in 1931, then at Michigan State in 1932. He spent 1933–1938 on the staff at Fordham under head coach Jim Crowley, a halfback in Notre Dame's Four Horsemen backfield of 1924. From 1935 to 1937, Leahy's Fordham Ram line earned fame as the Seven Blocks of Granite, one of whom was future legendary Green Bay Packer coach Vince Lombardi.

In 1939 Leahy moved to Boston College for his first head coaching gig and guided the Eagles through the greatest two-year run in school history, with a record of 20–2 and a 19–13 victory over Tennessee in the 1941 Sugar Bowl. The Volunteers, coached by the legendary Bob Neyland, had not lost a regular-season game in more than three years, and Leahy's win that day propelled him to the head coach's office at his alma mater.

In 1941, his inaugural season at Notre Dame, the Fighting Irish finished 8–0–1 with a third-place national ranking, and Leahy was named Coach of the Year. Two years later, in 1943, the Fighting Irish were national champions by unanimous decision. That 1943 team featured Notre Dame's first Heisman Trophy winner—quarterback Angelo Bertelli, a.k.a. the Springfield Rifle.

Leahy spent 1944 and 1945 (World War II) in the Navy, and upon his return to South Bend the Fighting Irish seized ownership of college football. The Irish had dropped their season finale in 1945 and did not lose again until 1950. An entire class of Notre Dame students went through four years of school and graduated without the football team losing a game. That has never again happened anywhere in major college football. Those Leahy-coached juggernauts of the late '40s claimed three national titles (1946, 1947 and 1949), two Heisman Trophies (Johnny Lujack in 1947, Leon Hart in 1949) and two Outlands (George Connor in 1946, Bill Fischer in 1948).

In 1997, *Sports Illustrated* published an extensive article on what the greatest college football team of all time was—was it Notre Dame in 1946, or Notre Dame in 1947? Many of the game's historians believe it was Leahy's 1949 team. Sportswriters and fans at the time generally believed Notre Dame's backups could

LEAHY AT NOTRE DAME
87-11-9

YEAR	RECORD
1941	8–0–1
1942	7–2–2
1943**	9–1
1946**	8–0–1
1947**	9–0
1948	9–0–1
1949**	10–0
1950	4–4–1
1951	7–2–1
1952	7–2–1
1953*	9–0–1

*national champions
** consensus national champions

beat anybody else's starters. It was almost unfair.

Football practices at Notre Dame during the Leahy years, particularly the full-contact mid-week scrimmages, were so grueling that to the players the games themselves were days off. Leahy drove them, and himself, relentlessly.

He addressed his players as a group as "lads," and individually by their formal given names—Frank Tripuka was "Francis," Ziggy Czarobski was "Zygmont." He would be quoted in the press before every season saying things like, "We'll be lucky to make a first down," then proceed to win another national title. He refused to run up gaudy scores against his opponents.

The Master remained at Notre Dame through the 1953 season before retiring for health reasons. More than half of his teams finished undefeated, and five won national championships. He produced 20 consensus All-Americans and four Heisman Trophy winners (Bertelli, Lujack, Hart and Johnny Lattner in 1953). Leahy was inducted into the National Football Foundation Hall of Fame in 1970.

Ara Parseghian
1964–1974

Notre Dame went 2–7 in 1963. Ara Parseghian arrived in 1964 and came within a minute and a half of 10–0 and a national title in his first season.

Parseghian cut his teeth as an assistant from 1950 to 1955 on Woody Hayes' staff at Miami, Ohio, his alma mater. He was the head coach at Northwestern for eight years (1956–1963) before arriving at Notre Dame. His Wildcat teams played the Irish four times and won all four. So they hired him.

After the remarkable turnaround of 1964, Ara was named Coach of the Year. In 11 seasons at the Irish helm, he won two consensus national championships, in 1966 and 1973, and parts of two others. He compiled a record of 95–17–4. His winning percentage under the Dome of .836 is the third-highest of all Irish coaches who stayed more than two years—only Rockne and Leahy rank higher.

Before retiring after the 1974 season due to health reasons, Parseghian produced three bowl champions (1971 Cotton, 1973 Sugar, 1975 Orange), 21 consensus All-Americans and a Heisman Trophy winner—quarterback John Huarte in 1964. Ara was inducted into the National Football Foundation Hall of Fame in 1980.

PARSEGHIAN AT NOTRE DAME
95-17-4

YEAR	RECORD	BOWL
1964*	9–1	
1965	7–2–1	
1966**	9–0–1	
1967*	8–2	
1968	7–2–1	
1969	8–2–1	Cotton
1970*	10–1	Cotton
1971	8–2	
1972	8–3	Orange
1973**	11–0	Sugar
1974	10–2	Orange

*national champions

**consensus national champions

——— Lou Holtz ———
1986-1996

Before arriving at Notre Dame, Lou Holtz had been head coach at William & Mary (1969–1971), North Carolina State (1972–1975), Arkansas (1977–1983) and Minnesota (1984–1985), and had fashioned himself as something of a program rebuilder. That's what Notre Dame needed in 1986, when he was hired. The Irish were coming off a 5–6 record in 1985, finishing the season with the worst loss in the program's history—58-7 at Miami.

Holtz's record of 5–6 in '86 wasn't an improvement mathematically, but everyone around the program could sense the wheels were in motion for something special. By his third year in South Bend (1988) the Irish were national champions, and Holtz was Coach of the Year.

Holtz coached more games (132) than any other coach in school history and won more than any other (100) except Rockne. At Notre Dame, Holtz coached 14 consensus All-Americans. He led Notre Dame to nine straight New Year's Day Bowl games from 1987 through 1995. Three of his Irish teams played the nation's most difficult schedule,

and five finished sixth or higher in the final Associated Press ranking.

Over the course of his career, he won 249 games, ranking him eighth all-time on the NCAA Division I-A list. And he was at his best against the best—against Top 25 competition he was 32–20–2.

HOLTZ AT NOTRE DAME
100-30-2

YEAR	RECORD	BOWL
1986	5–6	
1987	8–4	Cotton
1988**	12–0	Fiesta
1989*	12–1	Orange
1990	9–3	Orange
1991	10–3	Sugar
1992	10–1–1	Cotton
1993*	11–1	Cotton
1994	6–5–1	Fiesta
1995	9–3	Orange
1996	8–3	

*national champions
**consensus national champions

63

Terry Hanratty quarterbacked one of history's greatest teams—the 1966 Irish.

THE NATIONAL CHAMPIONSHIPS

There are almost too many Notre Dame national championships to elaborate fully on all of them. Eleven times, the Fighting Irish have stood alone atop the college football world, and 10 more times, the Irish have earned a piece of the title. National championships and Notre Dame have been virtually inseparable companions since Rockne arrived in South Bend.

———— Consenusus National Titles ————

1924

The 1924 Notre Dame team will always be known for the backfield immortalized in the game recap that Grantland Rice filed with the *New York Herald Tribune* the day after the Army game, the story that led off with these words: "Outlined against a blue-gray October sky, the Four Horsemen rode again."

Quarterback Harry Stuhldreher, halfbacks Don Miller and Jim Crowley and fullback Elmer Layden had been playing together as a unit since the end of their sophomore year in 1922,

and by 1924 they were a dazzling spectacle. In the words of their coach, Knute Rockne, the backfield was "a product of destiny." They operated behind a line known as the Seven Mules, featuring ends Ed Hunsinger and Chuck Collins, tackles Rip Miller and Joe Bach, guards Noble Kizer and John Weibel, and center Adam Walsh.

Another component of the team mostly forgotten by now were the shock troops, a complete unit of second-stringers that started every game and wore down the opponents for the first stringers.

The great 1924 team, Notre Dame's first consensus national champion, outscored its nine regular-season opponents 258–44. It beat Army 13–3, Northwestern 13–6, and otherwise was not seriously challenged. Following the season, Rockne convinced university officials to permit his team to travel to California to play undefeated Stanford in the Rose Bowl game. The Indians were led by All-America fullback Ernie Nevers and coached by the immortal Glenn "Pop" Warner. Notre Dame won the game 27–10, thanks to fullback Elmer Layden's three touchdowns—a three-yard run and interception returns of 78 and 70 yards. It was Notre Dame's first and only postseason appearance until 1970.

1929

"Fair. Just fair," was Knute Rockne's reply to questions regarding his team's chances entering the 1929 season. But that fall, junior Frank Carideo became a starter and established himself as the greatest quarterback in Notre Dame history, with the possible exception of Johnny Lujack years later. Carideo started for two years and won the national championship both years, as well as every game he ever started.

Rockne's Ramblers played every game on the road that year, with Notre Dame Stadium under construction. Some 551,112 fans turned out to see the 1929 Irish play.

Carideo was a unanimous first-team All-American that year, as was guard Jack Cannon.

Behind the running of Jack Elder, Joe Savoldi, Marty Brill, Larry "Moon" Mullins and Marchy Schwartz, the Irish dispatched all nine opponents on the slate. Savoldi made a name for himself in the Wisconsin game at Soldier Field in Chicago, with touchdown runs of 71 and 40 yards.

The season finale, against Army on November 30, was played on a frozen surface at Yankee Stadium. With the game scoreless in the second quarter, Elder intercepted a pass by Army's Red Cagle and returned it 93 yards for a touchdown. The Irish won the game 7–0 and the national title with a 9–0 record, playing the entire season without a home.

Rockne took his Ramblers on the road for nine decisive victories during the 1929 national championship season.

1930

In a way, the 1929 Notre Dame team was a precursor to the 1930 squad, which Rockne considered to be his best. Rockne's Irish finally had a home in Notre Dame Stadium. Carideo was back at quarterback and was a unanimous first-team All-American for the second straight year.

Carideo and fellow All-Americans Marchy Schwartz, Marty Brill and Jumpin' Joe Savoldi, as a unit, brought back memories of the Four Horsemen of six years earlier. The line was a formidable group led by All-Americans Bert Metzger, Tommy Yarr and Joe Kurth.

Notre Dame began the season 3–0 after a three-game home stand. Even after taking to the road, the Irish continued to roll. In Game 6, they trounced Penn, 60–20, when Brill, a Penn transfer, scored on runs of 45, 52 and 65 yards.

The Irish were 8–0 with Army and USC remaining. Schwartz scored on a 54-yard run to take a 7–0 lead over the Cadets. When Army scored soon after on a blocked punt, the Irish blocked the extra point, and the game ended in a 7–6 win. Second-string halfback Bucky O'Connor ran for two touchdowns, including an 80-yard sprint, against the Trojans in the 27–0 season-ending victory. Rockne's masterpiece finished 10–0 and repeated as national champions.

1943

Coach Frank Leahy's 1942 Fighting Irish finished 7–2–2 and returned only two starters for 1943. But that didn't deter this Irish team, as it finished with a 9–1 record after playing what may have been the most difficult schedule in school history. Seven of 10 opponents finished in the final AP top 13.

Angelo Bertelli had moved from tailback to quarterback the season before, as Leahy changed his offense from the single wing to the T-formation. Improvement was evident as the 1943 Irish increased their scoring by 156 points over 1942. In all, the 1943 national champions outscored their opponents 340–69.

Going into the final four games of the season, the Irish were rolling along unchallenged, with wins over Pittsburgh 41–0, Georgia Tech 55–13, Michigan 35–12, Wisconsin 50–0, Illinois 47–0 and Navy 33–6.

Two of Frank Leahy's legends, Angelo Bertelli and Johnny Lujack, were integral to Notre Dame's remarkable run during the 1940s.

Then the Marine Corps called up quarterback Angelo Bertelli, Notre Dame's first Heisman Trophy winner, for service in World War II.

Sophomore Johnny Lujack took over at quarterback and threw two touchdown passes, ran for another and intercepted a pass in his first start, a 26–0 win over Army.

The 19–14 loss to Great Lakes Naval Training Station in the finale marred the record, but the title was in place. Halfback Creighton Miller led the nation in rushing that season with 911 yards and joined Bertelli, end John Yonakor, tackle Jim White, guard Pat Filley and center Herb Coleman as All-Americans.

Georgia Tech coach Bill Alexander said of the 1943 Irish, "They had speed, power and deception in their attack, and they looked like one of the best teams I have seen in years."

1946

After World War II was over and the boys came home, coach Frank Leahy and Notre Dame took control of college football and would not let go. After dropping the 1945 finale to Great Lakes 39–7, the Fighting Irish did not lose another game until 1950. From 1946–1949, the Irish would go 38–0–2 and win three national titles.

In 1946, Johnny Lujack returned after two years of wartime service in the Navy and became, along with 1929 and 1930 starter Frank Carideo, one of the two greatest quarterbacks in school history. End Jim Martin, tackles George Connor and Ziggy Czarobski, guards John Mastrangelo and Bill "Moose" Fischer, center George Strohmeyer, and running backs Terry Brennan and Emil "Red"

Sitko, were among the foremost stars on this imposing lineup.

The 1946 Irish outscored the opposition 271–24, pitching five shutouts, including four in a row. But one of those shutouts was the infamous 0–0 tie with Army. Four Heisman Trophy winners played in that game—fullback Doc Blanchard (1945) and halfback Glenn Davis (1946) for the two-time defending national champion Cadets; Lujack (1947) and end Leon Hart (1949), who as a freshman backed up Jack Zilly in 1946, for the Irish.

The inaugural Outland Trophy was awarded in 1946, and Connor, arguably the greatest interior lineman in school history, was the recipient that season. Mastrangelo and Strohmeyer joined Lujack and Connor as All-Americans with the 1946 Irish.

1947

The 1947 Notre Dame Fighting Irish were likely the greatest football team of all time. Forty-two players from that team went on to play pro football, including some who couldn't even make the traveling squad. And they

played both ways back then, so that's just about four deep. That despite the fact that some starters, such as Brennan, opted not to even try out for the pros.

In 1947 Notre Dame outscored its nine opponents 291–52, never trailed in any

Bob Livingston still holds the Notre Dame record for longest run from scrimmage, a 92-yarder against Southern California in 1947, perhaps Notre Dame's greatest season ever.

game and only once allowed more than one touchdown.

Lujack was back at quarterback and won the Heisman Trophy for his 1947 performance, Connor, the reigning Outland winner, also returned, as did Brennan, Sitko, Hart, Martin, Czarobski and Fischer.

The Irish opened the season with an easy 40–6 win at Pittsburgh. After brushing off Purdue 22–7, the Irish pitched three consecutive shutouts, over Nebraska 31–0, Iowa 21–0 and Navy 27–0. Against Army the following week, Terry Brennan returned the opening kickoff 97 yards for a touchdown to spark a 27–7 Irish win. The following week,

Northwestern became the only team on the schedule to come within two touchdowns of Notre Dame but fell to the Irish 26–19.

The season ended with wins of 59–6 over Tulane and 38–7 at USC.

Six members of the 1947 team—Lujack, Sitko, Hart, Connor, Czarobski and Fischer— are in the College Football Hall of Fame, as is Leahy, their coach. *The Boston Herald* called the 1947 Irish "the greatest Notre Dame squad of all time. Its third string could whip most varsities." According to Grantland Rice: "College football never before has known a team so big, so fast and so powerful." He forgot to mention deep.

1949

"We'll have the worst team Notre Dame has ever had." Thus spake coach Frank Leahy before the 1949 season. The Fighting Irish had won national titles in 1946 and 1947 and finished second in 1948. They hadn't been beaten in three years and were about to make it four.

Junior Bob Williams quarterbacked the club in 1949 and made first-team All-American, as did fullback Emil "Six-yard" Sitko, end Leon Hart and Jim Martin, who had moved from end to tackle for his senior year. Hart won the Heisman Trophy as a senior that year, something no other lineman has been able to accomplish since then.

The 1949 Irish beat their 10 opponents by an average score of 36–9. The Irish took over the No. 1 ranking after a 35–12 win over Purdue in Week 3, celebrated with a 46–7 thumping of fourth-ranked Tulane in Week 4 and easily held on to the top spot for the remainder of the season.

According to Braven Dwyer of the *Los Angeles Times* following the 32–0 Irish win over USC on November 26, "Make mistakes against the average team and you're in trouble. Make mistakes against Notre Dame and it's suicide. Even a perfect team couldn't have turned back this great Irish squad."

SMU and its great backfield starring Doak Walker, who had won the Heisman Trophy the previous season, and Kyle Rote, gave Notre Dame its only real challenge of the season in the December 3 finale, but the Irish still prevailed 27–20.

"It's the greatest college team I've ever seen." This from the immortal Red Grange regarding the 1949 Fighting Irish.

Notre Dame guard John Helwig (No. 49) knocks down a North Carolina pass on the goal line in the second period of the Notre Dame–North Carolina game at Yankee Stadium on November 12, 1949.

1966 Fighting Irish offense

1966

In 1964, his first season, Ara Parseghian had come within a minute and a half of the national championship, and in 1966 he continued a tradition of Notre Dame coaches capturing the title in their third year.

Quarterback Terry Hanratty and end Jim Seymour opened the 1966 campaign as starters. In the nationally televised season opener against eighth-ranked Purdue, Hanratty and Seymour connected on 13 passes for 276 yards and three touchdowns and acquired the nickname Touchdown Twins.

The All-America teams were heavily populated with Irish players that fall, including Hanratty, Seymour, halfback Nick Eddy, fullback Larry Conjar, offensive tackle Paul Seiler, guard Tom Regner, center George Goeddeke, defensive end Alan Page, defensive tackles Kevin Hardy and Pete Duranko, linebacker Jim Lynch and safety Tom Schoen. Eddy, Regner, Page and Lynch were consensus first-team picks. Eddy came in third in that year's Heisman race.

Halfback Rocky Bleier and guard Bob Kuechenberg were future NFL stars

1966 Fighting Irish defense

hidden amid the greatness on the 1966 Irish roster.

The Irish shut out six opponents that season, including three in a row in October.

Ara's Irish took their 8–0 record and No. 1 ranking to East Lansing for the enormously hyped showdown with Michigan State. Eddy was unavailable for the contest with a shoulder injury, Spartan defensive end Bubba Smith had knocked Hanratty and Goeddeke out of the game in the first quarter, and the game ended in a 10–10 tie. After the game, Smith said of

the Irish, "Man, those cats hit and stick to you. That game was rough."

"The Super Bowl was not as big as that Michigan State–Notre Dame game," said Lynch, who played in Super Bowl VI as a linebacker for the Kansas City Chiefs.

The following week, the Irish traveled to Los Angeles to take on USC in the season finale, having left Hanratty, Eddy and Goeddeke back in South Bend, and rolled over the Pac-8 champions 51–0. It was all the pollsters had to see, and the Irish were national champions.

1973

The Irish won their second consensus national title under Ara Parseghian in 1973. That Notre Dame team outscored the opposition 358–66. Tight end Dave Casper and cornerback Mike Townsend were consensus All-Americans in 1973, with a half dozen or more youngsters on the club destined for the All-America designation the following season.

Junior Tom Clements quarterbacked the 1973 Irish. The offense was based on misdirection plays, with all four starters at running back sharing the load. Fullback Wayne Bullock led the way with 752 rushing yards, halfback Art Best followed with 700, halfback Eric Penick added 586, and Clements pitched in with 360.

The Irish were 5–0 and ranked eighth in the nation going into the game with sixth-ranked USC. Penick ran for 118 yards, 50 more than the entire USC team, and scored on a dazzling 85-yard run as the Irish snapped the Trojans' 23-game unbeaten streak with the 23–14 victory.

Notre Dame cruised through the rest of the slate before traveling to New Orleans for the Sugar Bowl matchup with Alabama on New Year's Eve night. What transpired was one of the greatest games in history, pitting Bear Bryant's top-ranked Crimson Tide against Parseghian's second-ranked Irish.

"It was the kind of game you could sink your teeth into," Bryant said.

The lead changed hands six times before Notre Dame prevailed 24–23 and claimed the school's ninth consensus national championship.

1977

Dan Devine got into the national title act as Notre Dame's coach in his third year at the helm, 1973. There were some all-time greats on that year's Irish team, players such as tight end Ken MacAfee, guard Ernie Hughes, defensive ends Ross Browner and Willie Fry, linebacker Bob Golic, and defensive backs Jim Browner and Luther Bradley.

And, oh yes, quarterback Joe Montana.

Montana did not take over as the starter until Game 4, after there had already been a

Joe Cool and the 1977 Irish earned Notre Dame its 10th national championship.

loss on the record, 20–13, in Week 2 at Ole Miss. But the following Saturday, with the Irish trailing Purdue 24–14, Montana came off the bench to throw for 154 yards and a touchdown, leading the Gold and Blue to the 31–24 win. From that point on, he never relinquished the job.

The Irish were ranked 11th nationally when USC came to town. Wearing green jerseys for the fifth-ranked Trojans, Notre Dame rolled to a 49–19 win and never looked

back. The regular season ended with a 48–10 trouncing of Miami.

On New Year's Day 1978, Notre Dame met top-ranked Texas in the Cotton Bowl. After finishing the first quarter tied at 3–3, the Irish exploded for three touchdowns in the second quarter and never looked back, bottling up the Longhorns' Heisman Trophy–winning running back, Earl Campbell, in a 38–10 romp. National title No. 10 was in the books.

1988

Almost predictably, Notre Dame won the national title in Lou Holtz's third year on the job. But during the preseason, it didn't seem all that likely. There were no line starters back on either offense or defense, and 1987 Heisman Trophy winner Tim Brown had just graduated.

Even though there were all new starters on both lines, the offensive backfield—quarterback Tony Rice, fullback Anthony Johnson and tailback Mark Green—returned intact, and there was a wealth of great linebackers, particularly Ned Bolcar and All-Americans Michael Stonebreaker and Wes Pritchett. Flanker Ricky Watters, offensive tackle Andy Heck, defensive end Frank Stams and nose tackle Chris Zorich also graced the All-America teams of 1988.

The season began with a thrilling 19–17 win over ninth-ranked Michigan, propelling the Fighting Irish from 13th to eighth in the AP poll. On October 15, No. 1–ranked Miami came to Notre Dame Stadium and left on the short end of a 31–30 score. Irish safety Pat Terrell knocked down a two-point conversion pass by Miami quarterback Steve Walsh with 45 seconds remaining to preserve the win.

By November, the Irish had claimed the top spot. In the finale, they went west, to the Los Angeles Coliseum, for the annual showdown with USC. It was No. 1 Notre Dame vs. No. 2 USC. The Irish defense made life miserable for Trojan quarterback Rodney Peete. Rice scored on a 65-yard run, and Stan Smagala ran back an interception 64 yards for another touchdown in the 27–10 victory.

Next came undefeated, third-ranked West Virginia and their star quarterback, Major Harris, in the Fiesta Bowl. Notre Dame mauled the Mountaineers, holding their vaunted rushing game to 118 yards. The Irish held early leads of 16–0 and 23–3 and held on to win 34–21. The perfect 12–0 slate came with the national title. According to Holtz: "I think this team is underrated even if we are No. 1."

Tony Rice (No. 9), Ricky Watters (No. 12) and the 1988 Irish woke up the echoes for championship No. 11.

—— The Other Ten ——

1919–1920 Knute Rockne won national titles, or at least portions thereof, in his second and third years after taking the helm from his own coach and predecessor, Jesse Harper. These were the last two seasons for George Gipp, the greatest player in school history, and end Roger Kiley joined Gipp as an All-American. The Irish finished each of those seasons 9–0 with the Gipper playing his way into immortality. He averaged 6.9 yards per rush in 1919 and 8.1 yards in 1920 in addition to his exploits on defense and special teams.

1927 With Rockne still at the controls, the Irish won a piece of the national title with halfback Christie Flanagan, tackle John Polisky and guard John Smith all earning All-America honors. The season finale, a 7–6 win over USC, was played in front of a crowd estimated at 120,000, the largest in college football history, at Soldier Field.

1938 The Dickinson System awarded the 8–1 Irish the national title in 1938. With former Four Horseman Elmer Layden as coach, Notre Dame held its nine opponents to a combined 39 points for the season, shutting

out four of them. Steve Sitko quarterbacked the Irish that year, with Bob Saggau leading the team in both passing and rushing. The line was a powerful unit anchored by consensus All-American Joe Benoir.

1953 Frank Leahy concluded his coaching tenure with a bang, with an undefeated (though once-tied) campaign in 1953. It may have been the greatest backfield in Notre Dame history. Hall of Famer Ralph Guglielmi was the quarterback, fullback Neil Worden led the team in rushing, with Joe Heap and Heisman Trophy winner Johnny Lattner at halfback. Art Hunter was a consensus All-American at tackle. Leahy's final two games as Notre Dame's coach were victories of 48–14 at USC and 40–14 over SMU.

1964 Ara Parseghian took the coaching reins at Notre Dame on the heels of a 2–7 campaign in 1963 under interim coach Hugh Devore and had the Irish sailing along virtually unchallenged at 9–0, No. 1 in the nation after midseason. But the world came crashing down in the LA Coliseum on November 28. The 20–17 loss to USC that day, after Notre Dame

Jack Snow starred on the 1964 team that narrowly missed a national title in Ara Parseghian's first season.

had led the Trojans 17–0 at halftime, deprived the Irish of a consensus national title, but a number of services found the Irish deserving. Notre Dame quarterback Johnny Huarte won the 1964 Heisman Trophy. Receiver Jack Snow, linebacker Jim Carroll, defensive back Tony Carey and sophomore defensive tackle Kevin Hardy were All-Americans.

1967 The Irish were defending their 1966 national championship and opened 1967 with a resounding 41–8 win over Cal, but two losses in the next three games knocked Notre Dame out of the rankings. But Ara's Irish finished with six straight victories, including big wins over Pitt, Georgia Tech and Miami to close out the season. End Kevin Hardy and safety Tom Schoen were consensus All-Americans on a star-studded defense.

1970 The one blemish on Notre Dame's 1970 worksheet was a 38–28 loss to USC in the

It hardly seems possible, but Tony Rice and the Notre Dame offense may have been even better in 1989 than they were during the 1988 championship season.

regular-season finale. A 24–11 win over top-ranked Texas in the Cotton Bowl merited national title honors by Sagarin and a few other services. After all, coach Darrell Royal's Longhorns had won 30 straight games and hadn't been beaten since the second game of the 1968 season. The Irish had outscored their opponents 330–97 during the regular season, with three shutout wins. Quarterback Joe Theismann and wide receiver Tom Gatewood set school records left and right. Guard Larry DiNardo and cornerback Clarence Ellis joined them as All-Americans.

1989 Coach Lou Holtz's 1989 Notre Dame team was defending national champion. Heading into the finale at Miami the Irish were nursing a 23-game winning streak, having rolled through 11 straight in 1989. But they finally ran out of gas that night in Miami, dropping the 27–10 decision to the fired-up Hurricanes. The combined score of Notre Dame's 1989 regular season games was 406–173. Quarterback Tony Rice and receiver Rocket Ismail spearheaded the assault. The defense featured linemen Jeff Alm and Chris Zorich, linebacker Ned Bolcar and consensus All-America cornerback Todd Lyght. A 21–6 Orange Bowl win over Colorado salvaged a piece of the title.

1993 Kevin McDougal quarterbacked this unforgettable Notre Dame team that stood 10–0 after winning a titanic clash with top-ranked Florida State in Notre Dame Stadium. The following week, the Irish came out flat for the Boston College game and dropped what turned out to be a scintillating contest, 41–39, on a last-second BC field goal, and the AP eventually awarded Florida State the title. Offensive linemen Tim Ruddy and Aaron Taylor, defensive tackle Bryant Young and defensive backs Bobby Taylor and Jeff Burris manned the Notre Dame contingent on the 1993 All-America parade. After a 24–21 win over fourth-ranked Texas A&M in the Cotton Bowl, some selection services felt the head-to-head win over the Seminoles justified a share of the championship for the Fighting Irish.

"The Super Bowl was not as big *as that Michigan State–Notre Dame game."* —LINEBACKER JIM LYNCH ON THE EPIC 10–10 TIE WITH MICHIGAN STATE IN 1966

THE GREATEST GAMES

It's safe to say that the greatest games in Notre Dame history are also some of the greatest games in the history of college football. No other team has played in—and won—as many milestone games as the Fighting Irish. Many of those games changed college football history forever. Here is a small sample of that record of achievement.

NOTRE DAME 35, ARMY 13
NOVEMBER 1, 1913

The forward pass had been legalized in 1906 and utilized primarily as a desperation measure by teams fighting to overcome late-game deficits. But on November 1, 1913, the passing game was used for the first time as a team's *modus operandi*. Notre Dame utilized it, and Army had no answer for it.

Coach Jesse Harper and the Irish arrived at West Point with 18 players and 14 pairs of cleats, and the Cadets were licking their chops. After Notre Dame fumbled the ball away on the first series, quarterback Gus Dorais decided to open it up, with end Knute Rockne as his primary target. Having spent all summer on the beach at Cedar Point, Ohio, perfecting their revolutionary technique of quarterback leading receiver and receiver catching the ball on the run with his hands, Dorais and Rockne sliced the Army team to shreds.

Dorais missed on his first two passes, but connected on 14 of his next 15, including a then-unheard-of 40-yarder to Rockne. When the Cadets were looking for the pass, Irish All-America fullback Ray Eichenlaub enjoyed vast expanses of running room.

The Irish returned home 35–13 victors, having exploded onto the national scene and having changed the game of football forever.

NOTRE DAME 27, STANFORD 10
1925 ROSE BOWL

It was the last game the Four Horsemen would play together, and the last bowl game Notre Dame would play in for another 45 years. Knute Rockne's opportunistic Irish would not let Pop Warner's undefeated Stanford team off the hook for its mistakes.

The Indians drew first blood with a 27-yard field goal and a 3–0 lead after one quarter of play. In the second stanza, Notre Dame's lean, slashing fullback Elmer Layden took over the game, scoring on a three-yard run and a 78-yard interception return to put the Irish up 13–3 at the half.

Late in the third quarter, Layden punted and the Stanford return man fumbled. Irish end Ed Hunsinger scooped up the loose ball and returned it 20 yards for a touchdown.

With the Irish leading 20–10 with 30 seconds left in the game, Layden returned another interception 70 yards for a touchdown to make the final score 27–10. Both of Layden's picks came off the arm of Stanford All-America fullback Ernie Nevers.

NOTRE DAME 12, ARMY 6
NOVEMBER 10, 1928

This was the "Win One for the Gipper" game. Rockne's 1928 team had been decimated by injuries and almost became the only losing team of his career. It finished 5–4, and if it weren't for some Rockne psychology before the Army game, it would have finished 4–5.

After pregame warmups, Rockne called his team together in the locker room. He told them about George Gipp, the greatest Notre Dame player of all time, who had died during his senior year. Then he told them about Gipp's deathbed request to exhort a Notre Dame team to overcome great odds and win a game just for him, "for the Gipper."

Good luck
from
Gipp

"This is the day, *and you are the* *team,"* —Knute Rockne said after pregame warmups, November 10, 1928

"That's one for the Gipper," —Jack Chevigny said after his score

"That's one for the Gipper, too," —Johnny O'Brien said after he scored

"This is the day, and you are the team," Rock said.

There was no way Notre Dame could lose that game. The Irish fell behind 6–0 in the third quarter but won the game 12–6 on a one-yard plunge by Jack Chevigny and a 32-yard pass from Butch Niemiec to Johnny O'Brien.

"That's one for the Gipper," Chevigny said after his score.

"That's one for the Gipper, too," O'Brien said after he scored.

The Irish lost their remaining two games, to Carnegie Tech and USC, but the losing record was averted.

NOTRE DAME 18, OHIO STATE 13
NOVEMBER 2, 1935

Notre Dame has been involved in some great football games over the years, but this one beats them all. Both Notre Dame and Ohio State were undefeated heading into the game, but Notre Dame was a heavy underdog. One sportswriter picked Ohio State by 40.

In front of 81,000 fans in Ohio Stadium, the Buckeyes took a 13–0 halftime lead. The dire predictions appeared to be accurate. The Irish attack had been completely stunted. The Buckeye line made it almost impossible for Notre Dame to throw the ball, or even get a punt off.

"I've never seen a Notre Dame offense so completely stopped," said writer Francis Wallace.

Irish coach Elmer Layden, who had been the fullback of the Four Horsemen backfield, decided to start the second string in the second half. In the third quarter, Notre Dame backup halfback Andy Pilney caught fire. The score was still 13–0 after three quarters, but the Irish were on the Ohio State 12.

On the first play of the fourth quarter, Pilney hit Francis Gaul with a pass to the 2, and from there Steve Miller scored on the next play to make the score 13–6.

On the next Notre Dame possession, Miller fumbled into the end zone, where Ohio State recovered for a touchback. But the Irish weren't finished.

Notre Dame took possession on its own 20 with three minutes to go. Some dazzling runs by Pilney and a 33-yard touchdown pass from Pilney to Mike Layden brought the score to 13–12.

Coach Layden called for an onside kick, which the Buckeyes recovered. Then the Irish recovered a fumble by Buckeye Dick Belz at

The Fighting Irish take on OSU in 1935 in one of the greatest games in college football history.

midfield. After a brilliant 30-yard scramble, Pilney was knocked out of bounds and out of the game at the OSU 19.

Bill Shakespeare came into the game for Pilney with less than half a minute left and threw a pass that was almost intercepted by Belz, who could have redeemed himself for his earlier miscue. On the next play, Shakespeare threw the winning touchdown pass to end Wayne Millner, and the Irish escaped Columbus with the unforgettable 18–13 victory.

Even with Heisman Trophy winners all over the field, the 1946 Notre Dame–Army showdown failed to produce any points.

NOTRE DAME 0, ARMY 0
NOVEMBER 9, 1946

World War II had ended the previous year. Army had won 25 straight games and two straight national titles. Army had beaten the Irish 59–0 in 1944 and 48–0 in 1945. But Notre Dame coach Frank Leahy and many of his players had returned from the service and were back on the football field. The Notre Dame–Army game had been sold out since June, even though tickets didn't publicly go on sale until August 1.

The Irish had plowed through their first five opponents heading into the Army game. "Fifty-nine and forty-eight, this is the year we retaliate," was the chant heard around Notre

Dame's campus the week before the game. The Notre Dame student body called itself the SPATNC—the Society for the Prevention of Army's Third National Championship.

The game itself was hard-fought and brutal, but it failed to produce a winner. Leahy and his Army counterpart, Earl "Red" Blaik, both went conservative, playing not to lose.

In the second quarter, Notre Dame drove to the Army 4-yard line, but turned the ball over on downs after two quarterback sneaks and two running plays to the left were stopped short of the goal line.

Army's great backs, Doc Blanchard and Glenn Davis, were bottled up all day—except for a single play. Blanchard broke free on one run, cut toward the sideline and had clear sailing. But Irish quarterback Johnny Lujack, who actually was a terror on defense, cut Blanchard off and tackled him by the ankles at the Notre Dame 37. It was said Blanchard could not be stopped one-on-one in the open field, but Lujack did it, and saved his team the loss. The Cadets moved the ball to the Irish 12, but Davis threw an interception. Irish halfback Terry Brennan returned the pickoff to the 30, and Army's scoring threat was stopped. And the game of the year ended in an unsatisfying scoreless tie.

NOTRE DAME 7, OKLAHOMA 0
NOVEMBER 16, 1957

Oklahoma boasted the longest winning streak in NCAA football history at 47 games. The Sooners had trounced the Irish 40–0 the previous season in South Bend and hadn't lost a game since they dropped the 1953 season opener to the Fighting Irish, 28–21. Oklahoma was a 19-point favorite entering the 1957 contest with the Irish.

The Sooners drove to the Notre Dame 13-yard line on their opening drive, but the Irish defense dug in and held. That was the deepest penetration the Sooners would manage all day.

Both defenses controlled the game until, with 3:50 left to play, Notre Dame faced fourth-and-goal at the three. Quarterback Bob Williams faked a handoff to Nick Pietrosante into the middle and pitched the ball to Dick Lynch around right end for the score. Monte Stickles added the PAT and the Irish held on for the 7–0 win.

Irish coach Terry Brennan credited his defense with the victory. The unit had held Oklahoma's powerful running game to 98 yards all day.

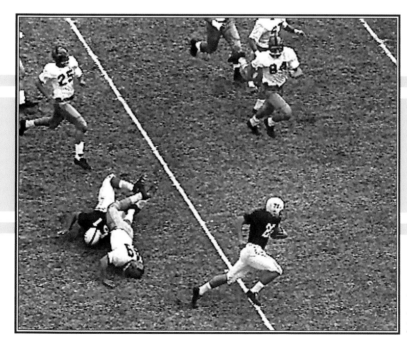

The Irish snapped the longest winning streak in college football history.

Michigan State coach Duffy Daugherty and Irish boss Ara Parseghian confer prior to the Game of the Century—the infamous 10-10 tie in 1966.

NOTRE DAME 10, MICHIGAN STATE 10
NOVEMBER 19, 1966

It was one of the most eagerly anticipated games in college football history—an epic No. 1 versus No. 2 matchup. Both teams were loaded with star players. For Notre Dame they included quarterback Terry Hanratty, split end Jim Seymour, running backs Nick Eddy and Rocky Bleier, offensive guard Tom Regner, center George Goeddeke, defensive end Alan Page, defensive tackles Kevin Hardy and Pete Duranko, linebackers Jim Lynch and John Pergine and safety Tom Schoen. Michigan State boasted quarterback Jimmy Raye, running backs Clinton Jones, Regis Cavender and Bob Apisa, split end Gene Washington, offensive linemen Jerry West and Joe Pryzbicki, defensive end Bubba Smith, defensive tackle Patrick Gallinagh, linebacker Charlie Thornhill and rover George Webster. They were arguably two of the greatest teams ever to play the game.

But the Irish played the entire game without Eddy, who finished third in the Heisman voting that year, because of a broken shoulder, and they lost Hanratty and Goeddeke both in the first quarter, compliments of Bubba Smith.

After a four-yard run by Cavender and a 47-yard Dick Kenney field goal, the Spartans led 10–0 in the second quarter. Coley O'Brien, Hanratty's backup, hit Bob Gladieux, Eddy's backup, on a perfect 34-yard touchdown pass to cut the deficit to three, then a 28-yard Joe Izzaro field goal tied the score at 10 on the first play of the fourth quarter.

With time running out, Notre Dame got the ball on its own 30. Coach Ara Parseghian decided to play it safe and go for the tie. It was a decision for which he was criticized. But history has proven it to be the right decision. His diabetic backup quarterback was tiring, and the 51–0 victory over Pac-8 champion USC in Los Angeles the following week, with neither Eddy nor Hanratty nor Goeddeke available to play, nailed down the 1966 national championship for the Irish.

NOTRE DAME 24, TEXAS 11
1971 COTTON BOWL

Coach Darrell Royal's Longhorns finished the 1970 regular season 10–0, defending their 1969 national title. They had won 30 games in a row and hadn't been beaten since the second game of the 1968 season. One of the 30 games in Texas' winning streak was a 21–17 victory over the Irish in the 1970 Cotton Bowl. The 1971 Cotton Bowl would turn out differently.

Irish quarterback Joe Theismann threw a 26-yard touchdown pass to Tom Gatewood and ran for two more scores, all within the first 16:32 of the game, and that was all Notre Dame needed in the earthshaking 24–11 upset.

Texas actually drew first blood with a 23-yard field goal by Happy Feller for a short-lived 3–0 lead. Then Theismann went to work, putting the Irish up 21–3 in short order. Texas running back Jim Bertelsen closed the score to 21–9 with a two-yard run, and a two-point conversion pass from Eddie Phillips to Danny Lester made it 21–11. Irish kicker Scott Hemphill split the sticks on a 36-yard field goal with the first half drawing to a close, and the second half began with the Irish leading 24–11 —and ended with the Irish leading 24–11.

The Longhorns outgained Notre Dame 426–359, but the Irish forced nine Texas fumbles and recovered five. It was Notre Dame's first bowl victory in 46 years; the Irish had abstained from postseason play since the 1925 Rose Bowl before taking on Texas in Dallas the previous year.

*Behind quarterback Joe Theismann, the Irish stunned top-ranked Texas 24–11 in the
Cotton Bowl to earn their first bowl win in 46 years.*

NOTRE DAME 24, ALABAMA 23
1973 SUGAR BOWL

It was a historic matchup—Notre Dame against Alabama; Ara Parseghian against Bear Bryant; No. 1 against No. 2; the two most tradition-gorged football programs in the land squaring off for the first time ever. And the game lived up to its billing, and then some.

A Sugar Bowl record crowd of 85,161 was on hand for the contest. The lead changed hands six times.

The Irish defense held Alabama without a yard of offense in the first quarter. A six-yard run by fullback Wayne Bullock put the Irish up

6–0. A botched snap on the PAT try kept it at 6–0. Midway through the second quarter, Bama went up 7–6 on a six-yard Randy Billingsley run. But Notre Dame's Al Hunter took the ensuing kickoff 93 yards for a touchdown, and the two-point conversion pass gave the Irish a 14–7 lead. A 39-yard field goal by Bama's Bill Davis made it 14–10 at the half.

In the third quarter, the Crimson Tide took a 17–14 lead after an 11-play, 93-yard drive ended in a five-yard touchdown run by Wilbur Jackson.

An Alabama fumble recovered by linebacker Drew Mahalic put the Irish in business on the Tide 12-yard line, from where halfback Eric Penick scored on the first play, and the Irish were back up 21–17. Early in the fourth quarter, Bama had the ball on the Notre Dame 25. Quarterback Richard Todd handed off to Mike Stock, who turned and threw the ball back to Todd, who loped down the sideline into the end zone. But the extra-point attempt failed, and the Tide held a two-point, 23–21 lead.

Notre Dame's Bob Thomas then put the Irish up 24–23 on a 19-yard field goal to cap an 11-play, 79-yard drive. With three minutes to play, Bama's Greg Gantt punted 69 yards and backed the Irish up on their 1-yard line. Roughing the kicker was called, but it would have given the Tide a fourth-and-five, so Bryant opted to decline the penalty.

He turned the situation over to his defense, hoping to force the Irish to punt themselves out of their own end zone and give his team another chance in Irish territory. But on third down, Notre Dame quarterback Tom Clements dropped back into his end zone and fired a 38-yard pass to backup tight end Robin Weber for the first down. From there the Irish ran out the clock on the rousing win and secured the 1973 national championship.

NOTRE DAME 38, TEXAS 10
1978 COTTON BOWL

When the 1978 Cotton Bowl began, there was one undefeated team in college football— Texas. When the game ended, there were none. Notre Dame forced six Texas turnovers and scored off five of them en route to the 38–10 rout of the top-ranked Longhorns to seize the 1977 national title for itself.

Longhorn running back Earl Campbell had won that year's Heisman Trophy, and he did rush for 116 yards in the bowl game, but they were all tough yards and they did little damage. Irish defensive ends Ross Browner and Willie Fry, linebacker Bob Golic, and defensive backs Jim Browner and Luther Bradley threw a lasso around the Longhorns.

After an exchange of field goals tied the score at 3 to end the first quarter, the Fighting Irish exploded in the second period for three touchdowns, on runs of six and 10 yards by Terry Eurick and a 17-yard Joe Montana–to–Vagas Ferguson pass. Texas cut the deficit to 24–10 with a Randy McEachern pass to Mike Lockett as time expired in the first half.

Ferguson added touchdown runs of three and 26 yards in the second half to slam the door on the Horns, and Coach Dan Devine celebrated his well-deserved national title.

A fierce Irish defense frustrated Texas all day long in the 38–10 Cotton Bowl rout that gave Notre Dame the 1977 national championship.

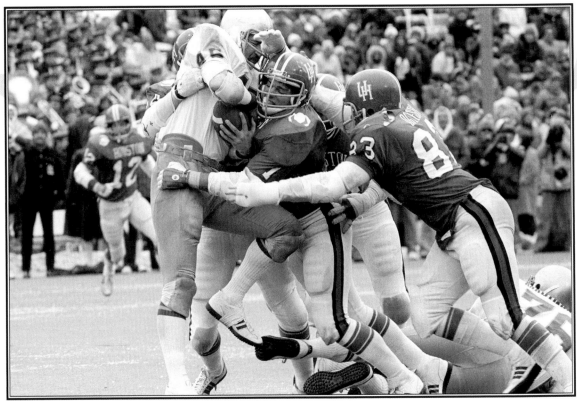

Things looked bleak on the icy turf of the Cotton Bowl. Then Joe Montana went to work.

NOTRE DAME 35, HOUSTON 34
1979 COTTON BOWL

It is known as the Chicken Soup Game. The Cotton Bowl game on January 1, 1979, against Southwest Conference champion Houston was Joe Montana's last football game as a collegian, and it was also his most miraculous performance.

The game was played in an ice storm. The temperature at kickoff was 20 degrees with an fierce wind chill. Notre Dame took a 12–0 first-quarter lead on a three-yard Montana run, a one-yard Pete Buchanan run and two failed conversion attempts. Then the Cougars battled back, scoring two touchdowns and two field goals to take a 20–12 halftime lead.

Houston tacked on two more touchdowns in the third quarter, and with a hypothermic Montana on the sideline unable to continue, the situation looked bleak for the Fighting Irish. But a heads-up Notre Dame assistant administered chicken soup to the ailing quarterback, bringing his body temperature back up to normal, and the Irish mounted an unforgettable rally.

With 7:37 remaining in the game and Coach Dan Devine's Irish trailing 34–12, freshman Tony Belden blocked a Houston punt, and freshman Steve Cichy scooped up the ball and returned it 33 yards for a touchdown. Montana hit Vagas Ferguson with a two-point conversion pass, bringing the score to 34–20.

The Irish defense forced another punt and went to work from their own 39 with 5:40 to play. After completing three straight passes to three different receivers, Montana swept left end for two yards and a touchdown. He connected with split end Kris Haines for the two-point conversion pass and the Irish were within striking distance at 34–28.

The Irish were driving again with 2:05 to play when Montana fumbled the ball away at the Houston 20 after a 16-yard run. But the Irish held and took over on downs at the Houston 29 with 28 seconds left in the game.

Montana ran for 11 yards, then found Haines for a 10-yard pickup. An incomplete pass intended for Haines in the end zone left two ticks on the clock. Montana called the same play, and this time it was complete, tying the game 34–34 as time ran out. Joe Unis' extra-point kick was nullified by a penalty, so he had to do it again. He did, and the Irish came away 35–34 victors in one of the most exciting bowl games ever played.

NOTRE DAME 31, MIAMI 30
OCTOBER 15, 1988

Defending national champion Miami took its 36-game regular-season winning streak into Notre Dame Stadium to face the fourth-ranked Irish. The Hurricanes had outscored Notre Dame by a combined 133–20 in the teams' previous four encounters, but the Irish were enjoying a resurgence under third-year coach Lou Holtz.

Notre Dame drew first blood with a seven-yard touchdown run by quarterback Tony Rice capping off a 75-yard, 12-play drive. Early in the second quarter, the visitors drove 68 yards in eight plays and tied the score at 7–7 with an eight-yard touchdown pass from Steve Walsh to Andre Brown.

Later in the second period, Rice connected with Raghib Ismail on a 57-yard pass on third-and-13 from the 17, setting up a nine-yard scoring toss from Rice to Braxton Banks. Less than two minutes later, Irish safety Pat Terrell intercepted a Walsh pass and ran it back 60 yards for a touchdown and a 21–7 lead. But within the space of five minutes, the Canes pulled even with the home folks on TD passes to Leonard Conley and Cleveland Gary.

The second half started with the score knotted at 21, and it got crazy. Miami's Bubba McDowell intercepted Rice at the Canes' 42, then on the next play, Irish tackle Jeff Alm knocked the ball loose from Conley, and end Frank Stams recovered to give the home team the ball. A Notre Dame field-goal attempt was blocked, and a Miami fake punt was stuffed by reserve quarterback Steve Belles.

Later in the third quarter, a 44-yard pass from Rice to Ricky Watters put the Irish in business on the Miami 2, from where Pat Eilers scored. A 27-yard Reggie Ho field goal extended Notre Dame's lead to 10 points, at 31–21. Miami's first possession of the fourth quarter ended in a 23-yard field goal.

Still trailing by seven with less than two minutes left, the Hurricane defense forced a fumble from Rice and recovered at the Irish 17. On fourth-and-six from the 11, Walsh found Brown in the right front corner of the end zone to cut the score to 31–30.

It never would have occurred to Miami coach Jimmy Johnson not to go for two points and the win. On the conversion attempt, Walsh dropped back and began to feel pressure. He lofted a pass toward Conley in the end zone, but Terrell stretched out in front of Conley and batted it away to preserve the one-point lead with 45 seconds left. Miami's onside-kick attempt failed with Anthony Johnson falling on the ball at the Miami 44, and the Irish ran out the last 42 seconds.

On the way to the win, the Irish forced seven Miami turnovers—three interceptions and four fumbles—and the 1988 National Title Express stayed right on track.

One of the most memorable days in Notre Dame football history. The Irish shook down the thunder with a thrilling 31–30 win over top-ranked Miami.

NOTRE DAME 34, WEST VIRGINIA 21 1989 FIESTA BOWL

The 1989 Fighting Irish football team was crowned national champions following a dismantling of third-ranked West Virginia, the only other undefeated team in the country, in the 1989 Fiesta Bowl.

Notre Dame quarterback Tony Rice attempted only 11 passes all day, but he completed seven of them for 213 yards and two touchdowns. The Irish mauled the Mountaineers with smashmouth defense and a punishing running game. The result was a 34–21 no-doubter and the program's first national title since 1977.

The Irish jumped on West Virginia and its star quarterback, Major Harris, early and never let up. The Mountaineers went three and out on the game's first series, and Notre Dame responded with a 45-yard Billy Hackett field goal, set up by a 31-yard run by Rice on third-and-seven, to take a 3–0 lead.

The West Virginia offense again was stuffed on three plays, and Notre Dame took over on its own 39. A 23-yard pass completion from Rice to tight end Derek Brown spiced up the drive that otherwise stayed on the ground—Notre Dame ran the ball on 16 of its first 17 plays—and Anthony Johnson found the end zone from one yard out on fourth-and-goal. The two-point conversion failed, leaving the score at 9–0.

After two more possessions, West Virginia still had not made a first down. Meanwhile, an 84-yard drive, highlighted by a 47-yard pass from Rice to Brown, ended on a five-yard Rodney Culver run for a 16–0 Irish second-quarter lead.

The Mountaineers put three points on the board with a 29-yard Charlie Baumann field goal capping off an 11-play, 52-yard march. But Notre Dame answered quickly, on a 29-yard scoring pass from Rice to Raghib Ismail. Time ran out on the first half with another West Virginia field goal, a 31-yarder, and the second half opened with the Irish in command, 23–6.

After Irish safety Pat Terrell intercepted Harris on the Mountaineers' first possession of the third period, Rice completed a 36-yard pass to Mark Green to set up a 32-yard Reggie Ho field goal. Later in the third, West Virginia drove 74 yards in seven plays, with a 17-yard Major Harris–to–Grantis Bell scoring toss cutting the Irish lead in half, 26–13.

The teams traded touchdowns in the fourth quarter. An 80-yard Notre Dame drive culminated in a three-yard touchdown pass from Rice to Frank Jacobs and Rice's two-point conversion. West Virginia closed the scoring on a three-yard Reggie Rembert run with 1:14 remaining to play.

The Irish outrushed the Mountaineers 245–141 and outpassed them 213–174. Of West Virginia's 19 first downs, five came on Notre Dame penalties. The score was nowhere near indicative of the total domination the Irish enjoyed on the field at Sun Devil Stadium that day, and Notre Dame's consensus national title No. 11 was in the books.

NOTRE DAME 31, FLORIDA STATE 24
NOVEMBER 13, 1993

The anticipation matched that preceding the titanic Notre Dame–Michigan State clash of 1966. It was No. 1 Florida State at No. 2 Notre Dame. Both teams were 9–0. Both sported 16-game winning streaks. It was Lou Holtz versus Bobby Bowden at the top of their games. The Joyce Center was filled to capacity and then some for the pep rally two hours before it started. Celebrities from Regis Philbin to Spike Lee to Roger Clemens were in attendance. By kickoff, some 700 media credentials had been issued. And the teams played the game of their lives.

After Florida State scored on its first possession, the Irish responded with an 80-yard drive, culminating in a 32-yard touchdown on a reverse by wide receiver Adrian Jarrell. A 26-yard touchdown run by Lee Becton put the Irish up 14–7. Coming into the game the Seminoles had given up only two rushing touchdowns all season.

A John Covington interception of a Charlie Ward pass put the Irish in business on the Florida State 23. It was only the second time all year that Ward, who went on to win the Heisman that season, had been intercepted. A third-down pass from Kevin McDougal to Michael Miller advanced the ball to the 6, from where Jeff Burris, on loan from the defense, scored. The half ended with Notre Dame up 21–7. The Seminoles hadn't trailed at halftime in 23 straight games.

A Kevin Pendergast field goal from 47 yards out made it 24–7. But the Seminoles came storming back. Ward engineered an 80-yard drive, capped by a six-yard pass to Warrick Dunn. With 10:40 remaining in the game, a 24-yard field goal by FSU's Scott Bentley made it 24–17.

Then McDougal went back to work, hitting Becton and Lake Dawson with completions for key first downs. Burris ran for his second score and the Irish were up 31–17. And then it got interesting. On fourth-and-goal from the 20, Ward fired a pass that bounced off the hands of a Notre Dame defender and into the hands of receiver Kez McCorvey, cutting the lead to seven with 1:39 left to play.

The Irish went three-and-out, and the Noles got the ball back on their own 37 with 51 seconds left and no timeouts. With three seconds left, Florida State had the ball at the Irish 14. Time for one more play. Ward scrambled away from pressure and fired a pass toward Knox in the end zone. But Notre Dame cornerback Shawn Wooden batted down the ball and the House That Rock Built erupted in pandemonium.

"I don't know how it looked from the stands," Holtz said after the game. "But I want to tell you I wouldn't want it any more exciting from the sideline. I can promise you that."

Quarterback Kevin McDougal guided the Irish to a scintillating 31–24 win over Florida State in 1993's No. 1 versus No. 2 showdown.

2005 versus USC

THE RIVALRIES

Two great rivalries have helped define Notre Dame football and have given fans many of their greatest memories. One of them happens to be the greatest intersectional rivalry in all of football.

USC

Beginning on Sunday, October 16, 2005, sportswriters and fans began to speak of the previous day's Notre Dame–USC football game as perhaps the greatest of all time. By the time the final gun sounded, not one player who participated in the contest had anything left to give. First-year Fighting Irish coach Charlie Weis wanted no part of the "greatest game of all time" dialogue—he was the losing coach in a football game and that's all that mattered to him. But two Trojan Heisman Trophy winners—quarterback Matt Leinart and running back Reggie Bush—were almost too exhausted to talk. Leinart was visibly shaken by what he had just experienced and by the Herculean effort it took to prevail over the Irish and keep USC's win streak alive, extending it to 28 games. Best game ever or not, it was one for the ages.

There is something special about the Notre Dame–Southern California series, the oldest and most prestigious intersectional rivalry in the country. Over the years, many national championships have been certified or lost based on the outcome of the game that was first played in 1926. The 77-game series has been replete with improbable endings, individual accomplishments and controversial plays.

It's a game that has enhanced the candidacy of Heisman Trophy winners. For Notre Dame they would be Angelo Bertelli, Johnny Lujack, Leon Hart, John Lattner, Paul Hornung, John Huarte and Tim Brown. For USC the names are Mike Garrett, O.J. Simpson, Charles White, Marcus Allen, Carson Palmer, Leinart and Bush.

It's a game that has matched the skill and knowledge of famous and legendary coaches: Notre Dame's Knute Rockne, Frank Leahy and Ara Parseghian, and USC's Howard Jones, John McKay and John Robinson.

It's a game that attracted the largest crowd in the history of college football, an estimated 120,000 for the 1927 meeting at Soldier Field in Chicago. The 1947 game at the Los Angeles Coliseum drew 104,953, still a record for that venerable stadium.

Yet, if it hadn't been for the persuasiveness of the bride of a young USC graduate manager and the wife of an immortal coach, there might not have been a Notre Dame–Southern California rivalry.

In 1925, Notre Dame was already an established college football power under Rockne. On January 1 that year, the Fighting Irish with the Four Horsemen had galloped over Stanford 27–10 in the Rose Bowl game.

USC had emerged in the 1920s as a formidable football force on the West Coast but was not recognized nationally.

Gwynn Wilson, USC's graduate manager of athletics at the time, recalled the unique circumstances that resulted in the start of the storied series.

"I knew that Notre Dame was going to break its series with Nebraska (after the 1925 game) and that there would be an opening on its schedule," Wilson said. "Notre Dame was to play Nebraska on Thanksgiving Day, and I thought if I went back there and talked to Rockne, there might be a chance for us to get a game with them next year."

Wilson had an ally in Howard Jones, who had been hired in 1925 and wanted to make a national impact. While coaching at Iowa in 1921, his team had snapped a 22-game Notre Dame unbeaten streak. He had agreed to give Rockne a rematch sometime. It wouldn't be at Iowa, though.

It was Wilson's notion to establish a home-and-home series with the Irish. However, he had to convince Harold Stonier, who was USC's

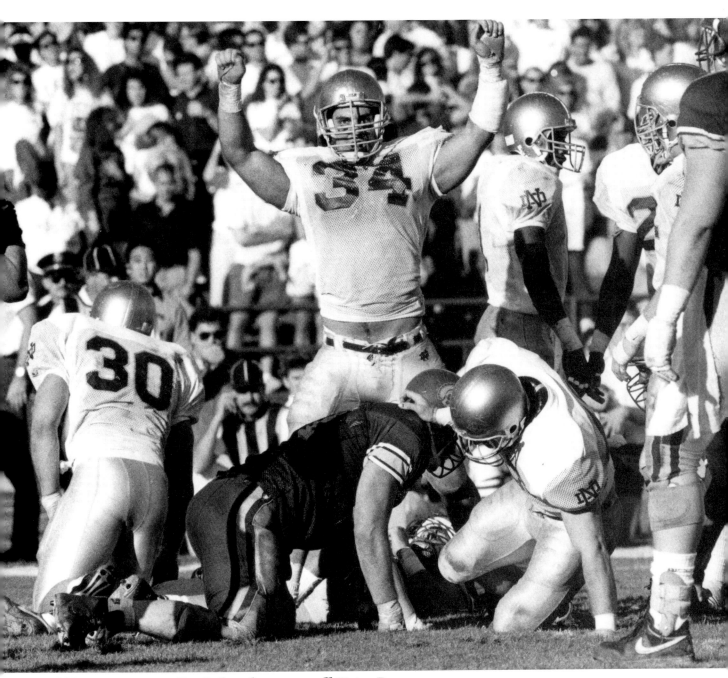

1988's No. 1 versus No. 2 showdown was all Notre Dame.

executive secretary and number two man in the administration.

Wilson didn't have to do much convincing, because Stonier believed it was about time that USC, then a growing university, should try to become nationally prominent in football.

USC had played few intersectional games, the most notable being a 14–3 win over Penn State in the Rose Bowl in 1923, and hadn't traveled east.

Stonier agreed to Wilson's plan to meet Rockne, but the 26-year-old graduate manager had still another request.

"I asked Harold if it would be all right to take my wife along, because we had been married only six months," Wilson said. "Those things weren't being done in those days. We didn't have big expense accounts but Stonier agreed."

So Wilson and his bride, Marion, took Southern Pacific's Sunset Limited to Lincoln and a rendezvous with Rockne.

"I went to the hotel where the Notre Dame team was staying, but Rockne told me he didn't have enough time to talk about my proposal there," Wilson said. "He said he'd get a ticket to Chicago for me and my wife and he'd talk to me about it on the train."

It didn't help Wilson's cause that Notre Dame was shut out by Nebraska 17–0. Nonetheless, the Wilsons were still hopeful.

"I really didn't get a chance to talk to Rockne until the afternoon after the game, when we went into the observation car," Wilson said. "He told me that he couldn't meet Southern Cal because Notre Dame was already traveling too much, and the team had gotten the nickname of Ramblers, which he didn't like. He also said he was now getting some games with the Big Ten.

"I thought the whole thing was off, but as Rock and I talked, Marion was with Mrs. Rockne, Bonnie, in her compartment. Marion told Bonnie how nice Southern California was and how hospitable the people were.

"Well, when Rock went back to the compartment, Bonnie talked him into the game. He came out, looked me up and said, 'What

kind of proposition do you have?' I said, 'We'll give you a $20,000 guarantee.' He said he would talk to Father Matthew J. Walsh (Notre Dame president). He did, and the series was on, with the first game to be played on December 4, 1926.

"But if it hadn't been for Mrs. Wilson talking to Mrs. Rockne, there wouldn't have been a series."

Rockne produced one of his strongest teams in 1926, one that seemed destined to win the national championship. The unbeaten Irish allowed only one touchdown in the first eight games. But Rockne wasn't with them when they met Carnegie Tech the week before the USC game.

Confident that his opponent wouldn't prove too troublesome, Rockne told an assistant, Heartley "Hunk" Anderson, to handle the team. Rockne wanted to see Army and Navy play in Chicago where he could scout the Midshipmen, who would appear on the Notre Dame schedule for the first time in 1927.

That slightly aroused underdog Carnegie Tech, which upset Notre Dame 19–0 in Pittsburgh.

Rockne was with his team when it traveled by train to Los Angeles, working out twice along the way, for the first meeting with USC.

The Trojans were as formidable as the Irish with an 8–1 record, having lost only to Stanford, 13–12.

The teams had contrasting styles. Notre Dame employed a backfield shift and misdirection plays. USC was a single-wing power, tailback oriented. Jones' teams became known as the Thundering Herd.

A sellout crowd of 74,378 saw the game at the Coliseum, later enlarged for the 1932 Olympics. USC led 12–7 late in the game when Rockne sent in Art Parisien, a 5'7", 148-pound senior reserve quarterback, with Notre Dame in possession on its 42-yard line.

Six weeks previously, Parisien had suffered a chest injury against Northwestern. Doctors had advised Rockne not to let him play. The Irish coach had brought him west only as a gesture of kindness.

On the short list of history's greatest games: Notre Dame–USC, 2005.

That thoughtfulness was repaid as Parisien, a left-hander, threw a 35-yard pass to Butch Niemiec. Then, with two minutes to play, Parisien found Niemiec again and threw him a 23-yard touchdown pass.

USC center Jeff Cravath, who became the school's 12th coach 16 years later, blocked the extra-point try, but it was inconsequential as the Irish won the first game of the series 13–12. The Irish took a quick three-games-to-none lead in the series, winning 7–6 in 1927 and 13–12 in 1929.

Rockne coached perfect-record teams in 1919, 1920, 1924, 1929 and 1930. He felt his 1930 team, which was his last, was his greatest. That fall, the Irish kept the Trojans winless in four tries in the series, winning 27–0 as Bucky O'Connor ran 80 yards for one touchdown and scored another on a lateral pass from All-America halfback Marchy Schwartz.

Frank Leahy coached Notre Dame from 1941 to 1943, and from 1946 to 1953. During his time in South Bend, he won eight of 10 against the Trojans (there was a three-year hiatus in the series, 1943–1945, during World War II. Leahy's postwar teams went four straight years (1946 through 1949) without losing a game. Though the Fighting Irish were perfect in 1947 and 1949, there was a scoreless tie with Army in 1946, and a 14–14 tie with Cravath's Trojans in 1948.

The 1947 Notre Dame team, arguably the greatest football team in history (though the 1949 Irish squad could give it a run for its money), routed the third-ranked Trojans 38–7, highlighted by a scintillating 92-yard touchdown run by Bob Livingstone, in the Coliseum.

One of the most unforgettable games in the modern era of the USC–Notre Dame series took place in 1964 at the Coliseum. USC, trailing 17–0 at halftime, deprived previously unbeaten Notre Dame of the national championship with a 20–17 victory on quarterback Craig Fertig's fourth-down pass to halfback Rod

Sherman with 1:33 remaining. The outcome enabled Alabama to win the title. Crimson Tide coach Bear Bryant showed his appreciation. He awarded Alabama letters to Fertig and Sherman. That made them the only players ever to receive letters from two different schools in the same season.

In the aftermath of that game, the Reverend Theodore Hesburgh, Notre Dame president from 1952–1987, congratulated McKay, saying, "That wasn't a very nice thing for a Catholic (McKay) to do."

Replied McKay, "Father, it serves you right for hiring a Presbyterian (Parseghian)."

In 1966, the Fighting Irish were coming off their famous 10–10 tie with Michigan State in that titanic No. 1 versus No. 2 showdown. The Spartans' immortal defensive lineman, Bubba Smith, had knocked Irish quarterback Terry Hanratty and All-America center George Goeddeke out of the game in the first quarter, finishing them for the season. And Notre Dame's All-America halfback, Nick Eddy, was already done for the year before the Michigan State game with a shoulder injury. So Parseghian and the Irish traveled to Los Angeles for their date with Southern California the following week having left three of the nation's top offensive players back in South Bend. The Trojans had already captured the Pacific-8 Conference title for the season, but the Irish rolled 51–0, with Coley O'Brien at quarterback. It was the worst loss in USC history. In the following year, McKay constantly reviewed that game film in his darkened office, searching for clues.

"We finally had to burn it when he wasn't looking," said Fertig, then an assistant coach.

In 1977, Coach Dan Devine momentarily delayed a run of Trojan dominance with a strategy that wasn't related to football.

His team wore blue jerseys while warming up for the game in South Bend, went back to the dressing room and reappeared in emerald green jerseys for the kickoff. It was a startling transformation, and the aroused Irish routed the Trojans 49–19.

Devine's successor, Gerry Faust, was asked before the 1983 game in South Bend whether his team would pull the green jerseys out of mothballs and try to recreate the magic.

"We'll always wear our school colors," Faust solemnly told a reporter. "I'm not opposed to the green jerseys, because they represent the Fighting Irish. But our jerseys will always have blue in them because that's the color of the Blessed Mother."

And the Irish were attired in blue jerseys coming onto the field. But they quickly changed to green jerseys—with blue trim on the sleeve—for the opening kickoff. Notre Dame responded with a three-touchdown win (27–6).

"I didn't lie to you," Faust told the sportswriter after the game. "Our jerseys had blue in them."

Notre Dame's 13-year unbeaten streak against USC began with three wins in a row under Faust, from 1983 to 1985, including a 37–3 rout in 1985. The 1986 renewal was Lou Holtz's first against USC as Notre Dame's coach. The Irish won 38–37 when John Carney made a 19-yard field goal as time expired.

The last time Notre Dame won the national championship, in 1988 with Holtz at the helm, the Fighting Irish were ranked No. 1 and the Trojans No. 2 when they squared off in the Coliseum. Both teams carried 10–0 records into the contest. The winner would head into the postseason as the favorite to capture the national crown. Holtz had sent running backs Ricky Watters and Tony Brooks home for being late to the team dinner the night before the game. With Rodney Peete as their quarterback, the Trojans outgained and out-first-downed the Irish, but Notre Dame prevailed 27–10 behind a 65-yard touchdown run by quarterback Tony Rice and a 64-yard interception return for another TD by cornerback Stan Smagala. From there, Notre Dame went on to defeat third-ranked West Virginia 34–21 in the Fiesta Bowl, securing its claim to the title.

From 2002 through 2005, USC won two national titles, and Trojan players captured three Heisman Trophies, largely as a result of their play against the Irish. Quarterback Carson Palmer took home the hardware in 2002 after throwing for more yards (425) in one game against Notre Dame than anyone else ever had and leading the Trojans to another Notre Dame opponent record (since broken) of 610 total yards. USC beat the Irish by 31 points that night. And again the next year. And the next, when quarterback Matt Leinart won the Heisman.

In 2005, Reggie Bush won the Heisman after running for 160 yards and touchdowns of 36, 45 and nine yards against the Irish. But the game had so much more than that. There were four lead changes in the fourth quarter alone. Late in the game the Irish led 31–28 with USC facing fourth-and-9 from its own 26. It was the Trojans' last chance to pull out a victory, and Leinart hit a streaking Dwayne Jarrett on a 61-yard pass play. With three seconds left, Leinart twisted into the end zone from a yard out, with an assist from Reggie Bush (the infamous Bush Push), for the 34–31 win.

Despite USC's recent domination, Notre Dame still leads the series 42 games to 30, with five ties.

—— Michigan ——

Mike Trgovac was a defensive line coach for Notre Dame under Lou Holtz from 1992 to 1994. But on September 15, 1979, the brawny, straight-talking native of Youngstown, Ohio, was a middle guard for Michigan, where he also served as the long snapper, under coach Bo Schembechler.

The Fighting Irish and the Wolverines were involved in the second game of their modern-day rivalry, and Trgovac later recalled the key play.

"We had played a great game defensively," he said. "They kicked four field goals even though our offense turned the ball over five times."

But with Notre Dame leading 12–10 in the waning moments, it was Michigan's turn to try a winning field goal. The Wolverines, who had beaten Notre Dame 28–14 the year before in their first meeting since 1943, were looking to go up two games to none in the renewed series. Amid the hysteria of Notre Dame Stadium's usual 59,075 sellout crowd, Trgovac leaned over the ball and placed his fingers on the laces.

The snap was perfect. Trgovac made his cut block and hit the ground. But, he said, "I guess I stayed down too long." Long enough anyway to enable Notre Dame linebacker Bob Crable, a man not known for his vertical leaps, to step on Trgovac's back and elevate just enough to block the potential winning field goal. At least that's the Irish version.

"I've told Crable a thousand times he didn't jump up and block anything," Schembechler said. "The kicker muffed the ball and kicked it right into his belly button."

Whatever, Notre Dame had avenged the previous year's loss and, more importantly, established what has become one of college football's classic rivalries.

Michigan has other rivals in Michigan State and Ohio State. But the Wolverines have dominated the Spartans for decades, and although Ohio State is still a big game, it doesn't have the national implications that Notre Dame does.

What makes the Michigan–Notre Dame game so great?

First of all, it's first. The game has always been the first or second of the year, which makes it the focal point of each young season. For the non-conference Irish, it's a sudden-death playoff atmosphere, because one loss can end Notre Dame's annual national championship quest. The message in South Bend the week of the Michigan game is: lose this one and play out the string.

Michigan needs the victory, too, if it wants to aspire to anything more than the Big Ten title.

"It sets the tone for the season," Trgovac said. "After we beat them (in 1978), I think it was tough for them to recover. And it kind of propelled us. It lets you know right away where you are as a team. In '91, Desmond Howard makes that catch (Michigan 24, Notre Dame 14), and we have a bad year (10–3)."

Second, it's the proximity of the two schools, which are a two-hour drive apart. That's one reason many top players visit both schools during their recruiting. Quarterback Rick Mirer grew up a Michigan fan but wound up at Notre Dame. Irish star Jerome Bettis hails from Detroit.

Then, there are the players and the unforgettable plays. The glare of Rocket Ismail streaking through the rain to return two kickoffs for touchdowns, giving Notre Dame a 24–19 victory in Ann Arbor in 1989. Mirer engineering a late 76-yard drive to lead a 28–24 Irish comeback win in 1990 in his first start as a sophomore—and winding up on the cover of *Sports Illustrated*. Howard making The Catch in 1991 to put Michigan on top 24–14 and himself in front in the Heisman Trophy race that he eventually won.

Last but not least, both teams have exciting fight songs. The Notre Dame "Victory March" is the most recognizable fight song anywhere, and Michigan's "The Victors" is also stirring.

"The Michigan–Notre Dame game epitomizes the best in college football," said Schembechler, who compiled a 4–6 record against the Irish before retiring after the 1989 season.

Schembechler wasn't just talking football games. Notre Dame–Michigan is a rivalry in part because even though one school is religiously oriented and the other public, both are high-rated educational universities that share common values.

"You have two big-time schools that understand where football belongs in the scheme of things," Schembechler said. "There's no hanky-panky in recruiting. Almost every top player has visited both schools. They're both classy institutions. You like that kind of competition."

Among players the competition breeds respect. And Notre Dame–Michigan has always been competitive in the extreme. For the Wolverines, it's at least on a par with Ohio State.

"It (Notre Dame) is the biggest game they play," Trgovac said. "They could win the Big Ten and go to the Rose Bowl, but if they don't beat Notre Dame, they don't think it's a successful year. It's that big a game."

There is one compelling reason to call Notre Dame–Michigan a great rivalry, and to

say they should meet every year—they are the all-time winningest programs in college football, in both total victories (Michigan leads 849–811) and winning percentage (Notre Dame leads .7435–.7425).

Having won three of the last four meetings, the Fighting Irish are creeping closer to evening up the series record. The 38–0 loss to the Wolverines in 2003 was the most lopsided score in the series and the first shutout since 1902. But former Notre Dame coach Ty Willingham was 2–1 against Michigan's Lloyd Carr, and Charlie Weis started in the Michigan series with a 17–10 win in Ann Arbor in his inaugural year at the Irish helm. It was a defensive gem by a coach known as an offensive mastermind and Notre Dame's first win in the Big House since 1993. It also snapped Michigan's 16-game home winning streak.

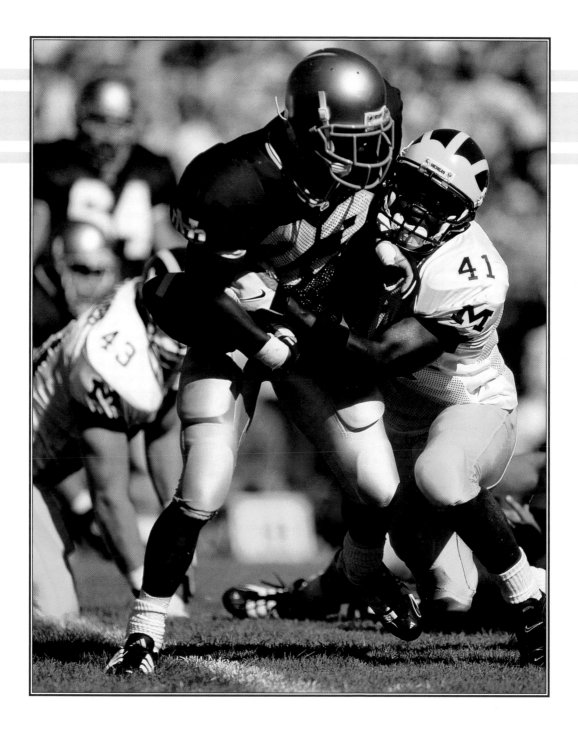

TALKIN' NOTRE DAME FOOTBALL

We thought we'd go straight to the source and let some of Notre Dame's greatest legends share their thoughts about Fighting Irish football.

"There were exciting games that whole year (1988). You play against the best, you were going to shine. These were all people who thrived on that situation. It wasn't really until the last game, against West Virginia, that we really started thinking about winning the national championship. We took the attitude of, 'Let's not worry about everything else. Let's just come out with the W.'" —QUARTERBACK TONY RICE, ON THE 1988 NATIONAL CHAMPIONSHIP SEASON

"Some time, Rock, when the team's up against it, when things are wrong and the breaks are beating the boys—tell them to go in there with all they've got and win one for the Gipper. I don't know where I'll be then, Rock; but I'll know about it and I'll be happy."

—GEORGE GIPP'S DYING REQUEST TO KNUTE ROCKNE

"He was a natural athlete... And he possessed the three most important qualities needed to attain greatness: the qualities of body, mind and spirit. He had what no coach or system can teach—football intuition." —KNUTE ROCKNE ON GIPP

"Notre Dame has one signal: pass the ball to (George) Gipp and let him use his own judgment." —CELEBRATED AUTHOR RING LARDNER

"I felt the thrill that comes to every coach when he knows it is his fate and his responsibility to handle unusual greatness...the perfect performer who comes rarely more than once in a generation." —KNUTE ROCKNE, ON GIPP

"9-3 is not good enough!" —A SIGN GREETING PLAYERS ARRIVING FOR WINTER WORKOUTS AFTER THE 2005 SEASON

"Brady Quinn is having a fantastic season. We have seen him for years; we have watched him grow up. He has always had games where he looked terrific but now he is just absolutely on the money. He is in control of his game and his team."
—USC COACH PETE CARROLL PRIOR TO THE EPIC 2005 NOTRE DAME–USC GAME

"That boy is going to make a great coach someday." —KNUTE ROCKNE IN 1930, IN REFERENCE TO SENIOR GUARD FRANK LEAHY

"I was forced to get a national schedule. I had to go someplace where I could get some ball games." —COACH JESSE HARPER, ON NOTRE DAME'S GROWTH AS AN INDEPENDENT FOOTBALL POWER WITH A NATIONAL FOLLOWING

Brady Quinn

Chris Zorich

"If anyone knows where there are four more horsemen,
I'll see him outside immediately." —KNUTE ROCKNE, SPEAKING AT A BANQUET A YEAR AFTER THE
GRADUATION OF NOTRE DAME'S FABLED FOUR HORSEMEN

"Before the game, Rockne came in and told us: *'I just heard*
that Army's going to kick you off the schedule.' Then he paused for effect. 'Well, they might be
able to kick you off the schedule, but they can't kick you off the field.' He used that as his theme
for that day, and we went out and won the game. The next day we picked up the New York
Times *and found out that he had signed a new five-year pact with West Point officials. We found*
out reading the story that he had signed it the Friday before the game—and he was telling us the
night before the game that they were going to kick us off the schedule!" —JIM CROWLEY, ONE OF
THE FABLED FOUR HORSEMEN, ON ONE OF ROCKNE'S MOTIVATIONAL PLOYS

"Once in a great while you can spot, *among (these) clumsy beginners,*
genuine talent." —KNUTE ROCKNE

"Psychology has its place in football, but not to the extent many football fans believe; otherwise schools would profit more by turning over the coach's job to the professor of philosophy...A smart running backfield, I've discovered, is better than any number of psychologists in winning football games."* —KNUTE ROCKNE

"Almost everybody was crying. The emotion of the game, the hitting and violent contact, was converted into the emotion of the locker room...the tears, the hugging, the trite phrases. Then Ara spoke to us, 'Men, I'm proud of you. God knows I've never been more proud of any group of young men in my life. Get one thing straight, though. We did not lose. We were No. 1 when we came, we fell behind, had some tough things happen, but you overcame them. No one could have wanted to win this one more than I. We didn't win, but, by God, we did not lose.'"* —EXCERPT FROM *FIGHTING BACK* BY NOTRE DAME FOOTBALL PLAYER ROCKY BLEIER, ON THE AFTERMATH OF THE GAME OF THE CENTURY WITH MICHIGAN STATE

"A good tackler will never reach for the ball carrier. He will run directly at him. A favorite phrase that we always give our tacklers is, 'Sprint to him, then sprint through him.'"* —COACH FRANK LEAHY

Rocky Bleier

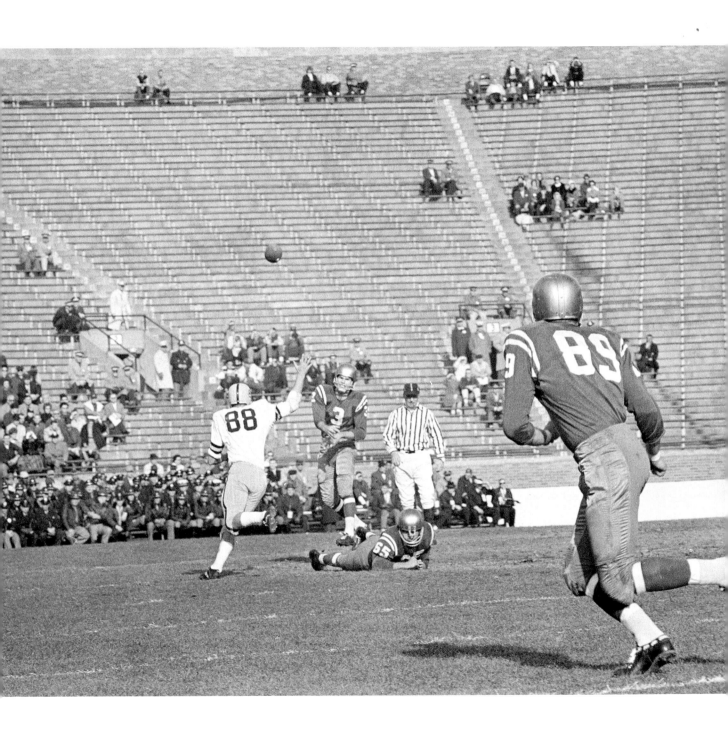

"You look at his interviews, the way he talks about winning, the way he approaches the game; I would have loved to have played for a coach like that." —NOTRE DAME LEGEND DARYLE LAMONICA (QUARTERBACK, 1960–1962) ON CURRENT HEAD COACH CHARLIE WEIS

"I've never seen a better intercollegiate football team than my boys who beat Southern Cal (38–7)." —COACH FRANK LEAHY ON HIS 1947 IRISH TEAM, POSSIBLY THE GREATEST IN COLLEGE FOOTBALL HISTORY

"After we lost the first one, Coach Brennan said not to worry, because every time you lost, you learned something. So I figured by the end of the season we weren't the best, but we sure must have been the smartest team in the country." —HEISMAN WINNER PAUL HORNUNG ON NOTRE DAME'S 2–8 SEASON IN 1956

"It wasn't until we were on campus for a week or so, solidly, that Ara Parseghian got caught up with the Notre Dame spirit. We were having staff meetings quite late at night. We heard this great commotion outside our window. There, in front of the Rockne Memorial Building, were hundreds of students, all carrying torches. They were singing the famous "Notre Dame Victory March" and chanting, 'Ara, Ara, Ara.' He turned to us with tears in his eyes." —PARSEGHIAN'S OFFENSIVE BACKFIELD COACH, TOM PAGNA

"There's pressure in every coaching job, but winning makes it a lot easier to accept. Fortunately, we have been winning. But like one fan told me, 'We're with you Ara, win or tie.' You notice he didn't say anything about losing." —ARA PARSEGHIAN

"There is a Notre Dame mystique that defies definition or description. It is something special in its combination of religion, education, and athletics. It is not only national, but international in scope. And there is a real tradition of achieving excellence whatever the odds...The first time I drove up Notre Dame Avenue after being named head football coach, an enormous sense of responsibility overwhelmed me." —ARA PARSEGHIAN

"Now, what can I say about my Notre Dame years? Paul Hornung and I had something in common. We both tied the all-time losing record for a season at Notre Dame. We both went 2–8. Now the difference is, Hornung got the Heisman Trophy and I got hate mail. But, I thank Notre Dame for giving me that wonderful education and for educating me, not only academically but for educating me socially."* —NICK BUONICONTI, DURING HIS PRO FOOTBALL HALL OF FAME ACCEPTANCE SPEECH

"It takes a big calamity to shock this country all at once, but Knute, you did it. You died one of our national heroes." **—HUMORIST WILL RODGERS**

"This was not only a great game for Notre Dame, it was a great game for college football." **—ARA PARSEGHIAN ON THE 24–23 SUGAR BOWL WIN OVER ALABAMA THAT GAVE THE IRISH THE 1973 NATIONAL CHAMPIONSHIP**

"There's no more pressure in any other coaching job in the country. Not everyone is cut out to coach football at Notre Dame. But I think Charlie is. That's why I think they eventually got the best person for the job even though there might have been some detours before it happened." **—GENE CORRIGAN, ON THE HIRING OF CHARLIE WEIS**

"We earned it on the field. We played No. 1 and we beat them." **—DAN DEVINE, AFTER NOTRE DAME'S 38-10 WIN OVER TOP-RANKED TEXAS GAVE THE IRISH THE NATIONAL CHAMPIONSHIP**

"If you're waiting for me to say it was a good loss, you won't hear that here. Losing is losing, there are no moral victories. What I did tell them was not to hang their heads. That was a slugfest, a street fight. That was a good football game." —CHARLIE WEIS FOLLOWING USC'S 34–31 WIN OVER NOTRE DAME IN 2005, ONE OF THE GREATEST GAMES EVER PLAYED

"The practice was very similar to spring practice. It was fundamentals all over again, and they were very physical practices. We utilized basically the same schedule we employed during two-a-days in August. The players get up at seven, have breakfast, practice, meet, have lunch, take two hours off while the coaches meet, have a kicking game meeting, practice again, then meet after dinner. The day ends about 10 P.M. with lights out. I don't think it is much different than a Marine bootcamp. One thing is for certain, when lights are turned out, they stay out. If they don't go to bed at that time, they are sending us a message that they aren't tired and we need to work them harder." —LOU HOLTZ, ON THE FIRST PRACTICE SESSION FOR THE 1989 FIESTA BOWL VERSUS WEST VIRGINIA THAT WOULD DECIDE THE NATIONAL CHAMPIONSHIP

"They did things to us I was afraid they were going to do to us. And there's no doubt about the great spirit they have here. I think it helps them. I do not think it hurt us. Their kids just played possessed." —FLORIDA STATE COACH BOBBY BOWDEN FOLLOWING NOTRE DAME'S EPIC 31–24 WIN OVER THE SEMINOLES IN 1993

Rhema McKnight—and yes, he did make the catch.

FACTS AND FIGURES

— Bowl Game Results —

BOWL RECORD: 13-14

SEASON	BOWL	DATE	OPPONENT	SCORE
1924	Rose	January 1, 1925	Stanford	W 27–10
1969	Cotton	January 1, 1970	Texas	L 17–21
1970	Cotton	January 1, 1971	Texas	W 24–11
1972	Orange	January 1, 1973	Nebraska	L 6–40
1973	Sugar	December 31, 1973	Alabama	W 24–23
1974	Orange	January 1, 1975	Alabama	W 13–11
1976	Gator	December 27, 1976	Penn State	W 20–9
1977	Cotton	January 2, 1978	Texas	W 38–10
1978	Cotton	January 1, 1979	Houston	W 35–34
1980	Sugar	January 1, 1981	Georgia	L 10–17
1983	Liberty	December 29, 1983	Boston College	W 19–18

SEASON	BOWL	DATE	OPPONENT	SCORE
1984	Aloha	December 29, 1984	SMU	L 20–27
1987	Cotton	January 1, 1988	Texas A&M	L 10–35
1988	Fiesta	January 2, 1989	West Virginia	W 34–21
1989	Orange	January 1, 1990	Colorado	W 21–6
1990	Orange	January 1, 1991	Colorado	L 9–10
1991	Sugar	January 1, 1992	Florida	W 39–28
1992	Cotton	January 1, 1993	Texas A&M	W 28–3
1993	Cotton	January 1, 1994	Texas A&M	W 24–21
1994	Fiesta	January 2, 1995	Colorado	L 24–41
1995	Orange	January 1, 1996	Florida State	L 26–31
1997	Independence	December 28, 1997	LSU	L 9–27
1998	Gator	January 1, 1999	Georgia Tech	L 28–35
2000	Fiesta	January 1, 2001	Oregon State	L 9–41
2002	Gator	January 1, 2003	NC State	L 6–28
2004	Insight	December 28, 2004	Oregon State	L 21–38
2005	Fiesta	January 2, 2006	Ohio State	L 20–34

Ara Parseghian was inducted into the College Football Hall of Fame in 1980.

—— Notre Dame ——
in the College Football Hall of Fame

NAME	POSITION	YEARS	INDUCTED
Hunk Anderson	Guard	1918–1921	1974
Angelo Bertelli	Quarterback	1941–1943	1972
Ross Browner	Defensive End	1973, 1975–1977	1999
Jack Cannon	Guard	1927–1929	1965
Frank Carideo	Quarterback	1928–1930	1954
George Connor	Tackle	1942–1943, 1946–1947	1963
Jim Crowley	Halfback	1922–1924	1966
Zygmont Czarobski	Tackle	1942–1943, 1946–1947	1977
Dan Devine	Coach	1975–1980	1985
Bob Dove	End	1940–1942	2000
Ray Eichenlaub	Fullback	1911–1914	1972
Bill Fischer	Tackle / Guard	1945–1948	1983
George Gipp	Halfback	1917–1920	1951
Jerry Groom	Center	1948–1950	1994
Ralph Guglielmi	Quarterback	1951–1954	2001
Jesse Harper	Coach	1906–1917	1971
Leon Hart	End	1946–1949	1973
Frank Hoffmann	Guard	1930–1931	1978
Paul Hornung	Quarterback	1954–1956	1985
John Huarte	Quarterback	1962–1964	2005

NAME	POSITION	YEARS	INDUCTED
Johnny Lattner	Halfback	1951–1953	1979
Elmer Layden	Fullback	1922–1924	1951
Frank Leahy	Coach	1941–1943, 1946–1953	1970
Johnny Lujack	Quarterback	1943, 1946–1947	1960
Jim Lynch	Linebacker	1964–1966	1992
Ken MacAfee	Tight End	1974–1977	1997
Jim Martin	End / Tackle	1946–1949	1995
Bert Metzger	Guard	1928–1930	1982
Creighton Miller	Halfback	1941–1943	1976
Don Miller	Halfback	1922–1924	1970
Edgar Miller	Tackle	1922–1924	1966
Fred Miller	Tackle	1926–1928	1985
Wayne Millner	End	1933–1935	1990
Alan Page	Defensive End	1964–1966	1993
Ara Parseghian	Coach	1964–1974	1980
Knute Rockne	Coach	1918–1930	1951
Louis Salmon	Fullback	1900–1903	1971
Marchy Schwartz	Halfback	1929–1931	1974
Bill Shakespeare	Halfback	1933–1935	1983
Red Sitko	Halfback / Fullback	1946–1949	1984
John Smith	Guard	1925–1927	1975
Harry Stuhldreher	Quarterback	1922–1924	1958
Joe Theismann	Quarterback	1968–1970	2003
Adam Walsh	Center	1922–1924	1968
Bob "Bobby" Williams	Quarterback	1948–1950	1988
Tommy Yarr	Center	1929–1931	1987

Career Statistical Leaders

Rushes: 889, Allen Pinkett

Rushing Yards: 4,318, Autry Denson

Rushing Touchdowns: 49, Allen Pinkett

Pass Attempts: 1,135, Brady Quinn

Pass Completions: 640, Brady Quinn

Passing Yards: 8,336, Brady Quinn

Passing Touchdowns: 58, Brady Quinn

Receptions: 157, Tom Gatewood

Receiving Yards: 2,512, Derrick Mayes

Touchdown Receptions: 22, Derrick Mayes

Points: 320, Allen Pinkett

All-Purpose Yards: 5,462, Julius Jones

Punt Return Average: 15.8 yards, Allen Rossum

Kickoff Return Average: 36.5 yards, Paul Castner

Total Tackles: 521, Bob Crable

Sacks: 52, Derrick Thomas

Tackles for Loss: 77, Ross Browner

Interceptions: 17, Luther Bradley

Allen Pinkett rewrote the Irish rushing record book when he strung together three straight 1,000-yard seasons in the 1980s.

The epitome of the Notre Dame student-athlete, receiver Tom Gatewood caught an Irish-record 77 passes in 1970.

—— Irish in the Final AP Top 10 ——

1. Eight Times—1943, 1946, 1947, 1949, 1966, 1973, 1977, 1988

2. Five Times—1948, 1953, 1970, 1989, 1993

3. Three Times—1941, 1952, 1964

4. Two Times—1954, 1992

5. Four Times—1938, 1967, 1968, 1969

6. Three Times—1942, 1974, 1990

7. One Time—1978

8. Two Times—1936, 1955

9. Six Times—1937, 1944, 1945, 1965, 1980, 2005

10. One Time—1957

GO BUCKS!